Innovative language teaching and learning at university: enhancing employability

Edited by Carmen Álvarez-Mayo,
Angela Gallagher-Brett, and Franck Michel

Published by Research-publishing.net, not-for-profit association
Dublin, Ireland; Voillans, France, info@research-publishing.net

© 2017 by Editors (collective work)
© 2017 by Authors (individual work)

Innovative language teaching and learning at university: enhancing employability
Edited by Carmen Álvarez-Mayo, Angela Gallagher-Brett, and Franck Michel

Rights: This volume is published under the Attribution-NonCommercial-NoDerivatives International (CC BY-NC-ND) licence; **individual articles may have a different licence**. Under the CC BY-NC-ND licence, the volume is freely available online (https://doi.org/10.14705/rpnet.2017.innoconf2016.9781908416506) for anybody to read, download, copy, and redistribute provided that the author(s), editorial team, and publisher are properly cited. Commercial use and derivative works are, however, not permitted.

Disclaimer: Research-publishing.net does not take any responsibility for the content of the pages written by the authors of this book. The authors have recognised that the work described was not published before, or that it was not under consideration for publication elsewhere. While the information in this book are believed to be true and accurate on the date of its going to press, neither the editorial team, nor the publisher can accept any legal responsibility for any errors or omissions that may be made. The publisher makes no warranty, expressed or implied, with respect to the material contained herein. While Research-publishing.net is committed to publishing works of integrity, the words are the authors' alone.

Trademark notice: product or corporate names may be trademarks or registered trademarks, and are used only for identification and explanation without intent to infringe.

Copyrighted material: every effort has been made by the editorial team to trace copyright holders and to obtain their permission for the use of copyrighted material in this book. In the event of errors or omissions, please notify the publisher of any corrections that will need to be incorporated in future editions of this book.

Typeset by Research-publishing.net
Cover design and cover photo by © Raphaël Savina (raphael@savina.net)

ISBN13: 978-1-908416-49-0 (Paperback - Print on demand, black and white)
Print on demand technology is a high-quality, innovative and ecological printing method; with which the book is never 'out of stock' or 'out of print'.

ISBN13: 978-1-908416-50-6 (Ebook, PDF, colour)
ISBN13: 978-1-908416-51-3 (Ebook, EPUB, colour)

Legal deposit, Ireland: The National Library of Ireland, The Library of Trinity College, The Library of the University of Limerick, The Library of Dublin City University, The Library of NUI Cork, The Library of NUI Maynooth, The Library of University College Dublin, The Library of NUI Galway.

Legal deposit, United Kingdom: The British Library.
British Library Cataloguing-in-Publication Data.
A cataloguing record for this book is available from the British Library.

Legal deposit, France: Bibliothèque Nationale de France - Dépôt légal: mai 2017.

Table of contents

Section 1.

Mapping the 'Global Graduate' landscape

Section 2.

Developing students' intercultural competence

Section 3.

Fostering employability in the classroom

Section 4.

Enhancing employability through digital tools

Notes on contributors

Editors

Carmen Álvarez-Mayo is the Languages for All Spanish & Portuguese Coordinator in the Department of Language and Linguistic Science at the University of York. Since October 2005 she has contributed to the development of foreign language courses, the curricula (including the Spanish L&LS degree), learning, assessment & marketing materials, and the VLE. Also a Spanish Lecturer at Leeds Beckett University, she has worked at Instituto Cervantes in Manchester and Leeds. In 2015/16 she was part of the organising team that brought the Innovative Language Teaching and Learning Conference to York. Carmen is a keen learner whose main interests are developing learning and teaching materials, new technologies, linguistics, literature, and equality & diversity issues. She became a Certified Member of the Association for Learning Technology (CMALT) in November 2016, is a member of the University of York Learning and Teaching Forum Committee, and works as a translator, interpreter, editor and voiceover actor.

Angela Gallagher-Brett is Head of Learning and Teaching Development at SOAS, University of London where she leads a programme of academic skills development for undergraduate and postgraduate taught students. She is a Senior Fellow of the Higher Education Academy and is an experienced language teacher and education developer with a PhD in Applied Linguistics. Her research interests focus on language learning and teaching motivation, employability in the curriculum, teacher research and partnerships between schools and universities. She has worked in UK-wide education development and internationally in European-funded teacher education projects.

Franck Michel is a Senior Lecturer at Newcastle University where he teaches French language, translation and interpreting, as well as French history, politics and society. He has a PhD in French studies and is a Senior Fellow of the Higher Education Academy. Although his field of research was initially focused on political communication and the study of electoral campaigns, he has since developed a strong interest in the areas of learner autonomy, feedback and reflective learning, in particular through ePortfolios. Franck founded InnoConf in 2010 and co-hosted its inaugural conference in May 2010 with his colleague Andrea Wilzcynski.

Authors

Ana Bela Almeida is a Lecturer in Portuguese language and culture in the Modern Languages and Cultures Department at the University of Liverpool. Ana is interested in the ways literature can enhance language learning. She has recently published a translation into Portuguese of a short story by Irish author Kevin Barry, accompanied by an introductory analytical study: http://www.ulices.org/projectos-investigacao/contar-um-conto-storytelling-en.html. Together with Dr. Idoya Puig (Manchester Metropolitan University), she is the coordinator of the Litinclass project, a research group working on the relevance of literature to the language class. Information on the project can be found at the Litinclass webpage: https://litinclass.wordpress.com/about-us/

Caroline Campbell is Director of Languages for All at the University of Leeds. Her background is in language teaching – English for Academic Purposes, Academic Skills, English as a Foreign Language, French, German and Japanese. The design of assessment is one of her main scholarship interests and ensuring that assessment is fit for purpose forms the basis of her feedback as an external examiner. She is IWLP representative for UCML (University Council of Modern Languages) and co-authors the annual "UCML-AULC survey of Institution-Wide Language Provision in universities in the UK".

Amanda Deacon is a Teaching Fellow at the University of Leeds. She teaches on French elective modules at all levels from beginners to CEFR C1 and coordinates the first year language programme for the French degree at the university. She also leads an undergraduate volunteering option, Linguists into Schools. She was educated in the UK, has a degree in French and African Studies from the University of Sussex and an MA in Lifelong Learning from the University of Leeds. Mandy has a background in teacher education and was formerly the Coordinator for the PGCE Modern Languages at Leeds.

Throughout her teaching career she has been involved in all sectors, from primary to higher education. She has also taught in France, the United States and Morocco. She has particular experience in teaching languages on vocational courses and is interested in Participation theory, creative and collaborative assessment models and ways in which technology can facilitate assessment and motivate students.

Sol Escobar is Programme Director of Languages for All at the University of Essex, but will soon take up a post at the University of Cambridge managing international language qualifications. She is also a Lecturer in Spanish (and occasionally ESL/EFL) with extensive experience in teaching EAP, translation and Spanish at all levels. An avid language learner herself, Sol has studied and taught in Canada, Italy, Spain, Germany and the UK, and her research interests are within the field of language acquisition, student motivation and engagement, language assessment, curriculum development, and language policy.

Theresa Federici began language teaching in HE and FE in 1998. She has specialised in teaching Italian and translation. She currently works at Cardiff University where she is a coordinator for Languages for All, the institution-wide language programme. Her research interests include student motivation and L2 identity, enquiry-based and process approaches to learning, and curriculum design for transferrable and professional skills development.

Mª Victoria Guadamillas Gómez holds a PhD in English Philology. She works as a lecturer and researcher for the Department of Modern Languages of the University of Castilla-La Mancha. Victoria teaches English and Didactics at the Faculty of Education in Toledo. Her main research areas are Children's Literature, English as a Foreign Language Teaching and Learning, and CLIL. She is the coordinator of the Language Centre English programmes in the Toledo Campus.

Susanne Krauß is a German lecturer and German coordinator in Languages for All at the University of Essex where she teaches German in face-to-face and online settings. Before she joined Essex in 2015, she taught German at undergraduate and graduate degree level in the UK, USA, and Germany, and has worked as a research assistant in a project on vocationally-based literacy training for adult migrants. Her main research interests lie in using technology for learning and teaching, vocabulary acquisition and material development. She has authored articles on foreign language vocabulary and grammar learning and the usage of digital tools and technology in teaching and learning.

Manuel Lagares is a Teaching Associate at the University of Nottingham, where he is a deputy Spanish language coordinator. His interest focuses in distance learning, collaborative learning, blended learning and the use of technology for pedagogical purposes.

Dawn Leggott is an Education and Language Consultant and former Principal Lecturer in Languages and English Language Teaching at Leeds Beckett University. She is passionate about helping young people to make the transition from education to employment. She gives talks in schools on the benefits of languages for life and work, runs university staff workshops on international student support and organises innovative employer engagement activities for universities, designed to boost students' networking skills and employers' links to graduates (www.dawnleggott.co.uk and dawn@dawnleggott.co.uk). In her free time she loves hill walking.

Cristina López-Moreno is a Senior Lecturer in Spanish Studies at Sheffield Hallam University, in the UK. Her research interests focus on the effects of the 2008 economic crisis on unemployment and on population movements in Spain. Another of her research areas is student migration and its impact on graduate employability skills. She is the author of España Contemporánea, a textbook on modern Spain which is widely used in higher education in many countries. She has also written a Spanish language textbook, Un Año en España, and in addition, she has presented her research in a number of UK and international academic events.

Sandra López-Rocha is a Teaching Fellow (Spanish) at the School of Modern Languages at the University of Bristol and coordinator of Year Abroad

Work Placements in Spanish-speaking countries. As a Fulbright Scholar, she obtained an MA in Intercultural Communication and was awarded a PhD in Language, Literacy and Culture from the University of Maryland, Baltimore County, followed by a PhD in Social Anthropology at the UoB. Her research encompasses: sociolinguistics (language maintenance and change); netnography (virtual communities and representation); migrant experience and adaptation strategies; and the application of intercultural communicative theory in the language classroom and in the Year Abroad.

Alison Organ started her career as a secondary school teacher before taking the Institute of Linguists' Diploma in Translation. After working as a freelance translator and language tutor for several years, she taught at the University of York before moving to York St John University full time in 2012. She delivers language modules at undergraduate level, as well as the MA in Applied Linguistics: Translation and the School Direct PGCE in MFL. Her research interests mainly involve the use of technology to engage language learners, and she is a Senior Fellow of the HEA.

Lucy Parkin works as a learning technologist, supporting both staff and students at the University of Leeds. Her main interests relate to matters of assessment, blended learning and staff engagement with technology.

Elinor Parks is a PhD student in Applied Linguistics at the University of Hull. She is also currently an LFA Tutor of German for the University of York and part-time lecturer of German and Italian at Leeds Beckett University. Her doctoral research explores the complexity behind the separation between language and content in Modern Language degrees both in the UK and in the USA. In particular, the research examines implications of the divide for the development of criticality and intercultural competence in undergraduates. She has presented at a number of conferences around the UK including Southampton, Liverpool, Sheffield, Leeds, Nottingham and York.

Alessia Plutino is currently a Teaching Fellow of Italian at the University of Southampton and an Associate Lecturer of Italian at The Open University. She has multiple research interests ranging from Computer Assisted Language Learning and Telecollaboration, to students as producers and the use of microblogging. She has been using Twitter to enhance communicative language learning and accuracy skills in Italian and has recently been using it as a powerful tool to transpose classroom communities into online learning communities and enhance spontaneous and collaborative learning outside of conventional classroom settings.

Idoya Puig is a Senior Lecturer at Manchester Metropolitan University, a specialist in Spanish Golden Age literature. She has published a number of articles on Cervantes and sixteenth century Spanish literature. At present, she is looking at ways of teaching literature through film and new media and how to make literary classics more accessible to the wider public. She is working in the Litinclass research group with the aim of developing new teaching materials and methodologies for the teaching of language through literature.

Sandra Reisenleutner is a Teaching Associate at the University of Nottingham, where she teaches German language and content modules about Second Language Acquisition and Foreign Language Teaching. Her project and research interests are in the field of collaboration in the foreign language classroom, in the application of the CEFR to language teaching and assessment and in task-based language teaching and learning.

Carolin Schneider is a chartered librarian who manages the self-access centre at the University of Leeds and has recently finished an MA in Technology, Education and Learning. She has a keen interest in how technology can support language learning, with a focus on independent adult learners.

Fabienne Vailes is Deputy Language Director (French) in the School of Modern Languages at the University of Bristol. She is also coordinator of Year Abroad Work Placements for all francophone countries. Before that, she ran her own company, The Language Experience, which provided language courses as well as workshops in Intercultural Competence to businesses both in the UK and in France.

She completed her undergraduate studies in France (Licence/Maîtrise Langues Etrangères Appliquées) and then gained an MA in Advanced Language Studies (Translation/Linguistics) from the University of the West of England.

Jocelyn Wyburd is the Director of the Language Centre at the University of Cambridge. She has run language centre operations in different universities for more than 20 years. She chaired the Standing Conference of Heads of Modern Languages (SCHML) before its merger with the University Council of Modern Languages (UCML). She was subsequently Honorary Secretary, Vice Chair for Education, and finally Chair of UCML, until the end of 2016. In these roles and as Chair of the national Advisory Board for Routes into Languages, she has championed the interests of all aspects of languages provision in higher education.

Foreword

Jocelyn Wyburd[1]

Graduate employability is a sector-wide priority in an ever more competitive and global environment. UK Universities already publish metrics related to the employability of their graduates, including by subject area and degree programme, alongside others such as satisfaction ratings. Such data can serve to attract applicants, but are also increasingly being used to rate universities on the quality of their degree provision. This is particularly so since the Government announced the introduction of the Teaching Excellence Framework for universities in England, whose outcomes will then link to the right to increase fees. For students facing increasing levels of graduate debt, it is also vital that they will be highly employable by the end of their degree.

In a context of declining numbers of students taking degrees in languages, raising the profile of the employability of languages graduates and enhancing their employability through their courses is particularly important. This may seem ironic, given the increasing numbers of students who choose to take language courses alongside another subject of study, often in recognition of the value of language skills for employability purposes. Language skills are indeed valuable. However, what comes through loud and clear in this volume, is that employers are arguably much more interested in a wider set of transversal or soft skills, which are implicitly developed in higher education languages students, or can be explicitly enhanced by educators. This is what *Enhancing Employability*, the latest in the *Innovative Language Teaching and Learning* series, focuses on.

Some chapters consider initiatives which explicitly incorporate employment experience (e.g. Leggott; Organ), while the majority explore how a range of innovations can develop skills which are transferable to an employment context.

1. University of Cambridge, Cambridge, United Kingdom; jmw234@cam.ac.uk

How to cite this chapter: Wyburd, J. (2017). Foreword. In C. Álvarez-Mayo, A. Gallagher-Brett, & F. Michel (Eds), *Innovative language teaching and learning at university: enhancing employability* (pp. xiii-xiv). Research-publishing.net. https://doi.org/10.14705/rpnet.2017.innoconf2016.648

© 2017 Jocelyn Wyburd (CC BY)

What is notable throughout this volume is the recurring concept of a failure of recognition of these by graduating students and prospective employers alike and the need for them to be more explicitly identified and articulated. The key buzzwords which emerge centre around the 'global' or 'transnational', 'value-added' graduate, equipped with transcultural skills and a global mindset. To these, in some chapters (notably Deacon, Parkin, & Schneider; Campbell; Guadamillas Gómez; Plutino) are added a focus on digital literacies and e-skills as intrinsically valuable as well as providing an additional dimension to cross-cultural communication. Three contributions (López-Moreno; Organ; Guadamillas Gómez) focus particularly on different aspects related to residence abroad – an experience recognised as one of the richest seams of transferable skills for languages students.

What shines through in this volume is that addressing employability dimensions need not (as I myself point out), require an overhaul of the content of higher education languages degrees and courses. Indeed, two authors (Almeida & Puig; Parks) make the case for an enhanced set of transferable skills coming from the study of 'content courses' which focus on literature and other expressions of culture and society. What becomes clear is that enhancing employability may require techniques to be introduced which help students to reflect on and articulate the range of skills they are acquiring (e.g. Organ), or to tweak assessment methods to incorporate these (Campbell). Several chapters also focus on the processes not just of language learning but of 'living' the use of a second language in real contexts and of experiential learning as providing the strongest basis for transferability of skills and competence (Leggott; Federici; Plutino).

This volume is a call to action for higher education practitioners to make more explicit what the unique range of employment related skills their students are gaining, and to assist students in owning and articulating this skillset through experiential learning and reflection. It makes a timely and welcome contribution to the sector.

1 "Innovative language teaching and learning at university: enhancing employability" – an introduction

Carmen Álvarez-Mayo[1], Angela Gallagher-Brett[2], and Franck Michel[3]

1.   Introduction

Welcome to the second volume in this series of papers dedicated to Innovative language teaching and learning at university. This publication follows in the footsteps of Cecilia Goria, Oranna Speicher and Sascha Stollhans, who hosted the 2015 conference at the University of Nottingham and edited the very first proceedings in the series, dedicated to the theme of "enhancing participation and collaboration" (Goria, Speicher, & Stollhans, 2016). InnoConf, as it has now come to be known, is a series of annual symposia primarily aimed at language-teaching practitioners in Higher Education (HE).

This initiative, originally launched in 2011 by Franck Michel and Andrea Wilczynski at Newcastle University, came to fruition to create a forum for all like-minded professionals eager to discover, share and disseminate good practices in the field of modern foreign languages. InnoConf has been met with great success over the years, and we are delighted to bring you this latest chapter in the series, dedicated to the very relevant and important theme of employability. As defined by Álvarez-Mayo (2016)[4],

---

1. University of York, York, United Kingdom; carmen.alvarez-mayo@york.ac.uk

2. SOAS, University of London, London, United Kingdom; ag62@soas.ac.uk

3. Newcastle University, Newcastle upon Tyne, United Kingdom; franck.michel@newcastle.ac.uk

4. See also Chertkovskaya, Watt, Tramer, and Spoelstra (2013)

How to cite this chapter: Álvarez-Mayo, C., Gallagher-Brett, A., & Michel, F. (2017). "Innovative language teaching and learning at university: enhancing employability" – an introduction . In C. Álvarez-Mayo, A. Gallagher-Brett, & F. Michel (Eds), *Innovative language teaching and learning at university: enhancing employability* (pp. 1-8). Research-publishing. net. https://doi.org/10.14705/rpnet.2017.innoconf2016.649

© 2017 Carmen Álvarez-Mayo, Angela Gallagher-Brett, and Franck Michel (CC BY) "[t]he term employability as we know it has been around since the 1980s, when international corporations, global competition/trade and technology cemented the foundations for a new economic environment. The influx of new technologies set the pace of change, and has been shaping communication and trade ever since. We live in a global world where IT keeps on developing faster and faster, highly impacting in our lives and determining the employability skills required for a successful career. It is essential to understand this in order to develop the motivation and prowess required to be able to keep on evolving alongside" (n.p.).

2. InnoConf16

On the 17th of June 2016 the VI Innovative Language Teaching and Learning at University annual conference: *Enhancing Employability*, was hosted at the University of York by the Department of Language and Linguistic Science and Languages for All. We were delighted to welcome as our keynote speakers Jocelyn Wyburd, Director of the University of Cambridge Language Centre since 2011 and Chair of the University Council of Modern Languages (UCML), as well as Lizzie Fane, founder and CEO of GlobalGraduates.com (formerly ThirdYearAbroad.com).

Speakers and delegates from across the UK and abroad were warmly welcomed to York and enjoyed a conference where educators and researchers in language teaching and learning came together to share best practices, reflection and inspiration, networking with like-minded colleagues and laying foundations for new and exciting projects and developments in language teaching and learning, driven by innovation and collaboration in higher education both nationally and internationally.

Jocelyn Wyburd opened the conference sessions with her keynote speech titled: *Transnational graduates and employability: challenges for HE colleagues.* Based on the research carried out for the British Academy's Born Global project, Wyburd highlighted "[the] demand for the skills [our] graduates in and with languages can develop" (Wyburd, this volume, p. 11). The talk also explored some of the mismatches between student perceptions of their own skills and what employers are looking for, and highlighted how we as educators can support students in developing their awareness of their employability. The paper appears in this edited volume in which Wyburd has also contributed the foreword, further sharing her expert knowledge and experience on the main theme.

In the closing keynote speech: *Promoting mobility and supporting your outbound students through social media,* Lizzie Fane reminded us how much communication and technology have changed in the last ten years and stressed how important it is to share and access information efficiently and be able to quickly find what you need in the relentless and fast-paced 21st century media/ technology world. Fane offered us a first-hand peek at GlobalGraduates.com, the new website which has now officially replaced ThirdYearAbroad.com; a most valuable tool, helping "students to become Global Graduates through study abroad opportunities, work placements, volunteering, languages and international jobs during and after their degree course" (https://globalgraduates. com/pages/about).

3.   Organisation of the book and chapter overview

Following on from the great success in Newcastle (2011), Bristol (2012), Manchester (2013), Leeds (2014) and Nottingham (2015), in 2016 the main theme of InnoConf was Enhancing Employability. The conference programme was varied and consisted of 24 parallel sessions, broadly organised into four categories:

- Mapping the 'Global Graduate' landscape.

- Developing students' intercultural competence.

- Fostering employability in the classroom.

- Enhancing employability through digital tools.

Together with Wyburd's keynote piece, this volume contains a selection of 14 short conference papers organised under the four aforementioned headings.

3.1.   Mapping the 'Global Graduate' landscape

Under this first heading, all contributors provide a distinctive overview of the skills employers are expecting from language graduates, and how language teaching professionals and their departments can adapt to engage with the working world and better embed employability into the undergraduate curriculum. **Wyburd**'s paper, presented in the previous section, is followed by **López-Moreno** who highlights labour market shortages of professionals with global skills. Reflecting on her own experience of managing international work placements, she illustrates how languages students acquire cross-cultural competence through international work experience but then fail to capitalise on this, preferring instead to focus only on their language skills. What students need, she argues, is to emphasise their qualities as global graduates with global mind-sets. **Leggott** shares in her paper some of her experience promoting student engagement and developing employability awareness, skills and knowledge among language students. Universities, local businesses and students of languages "can collaborate for mutual benefit, leading at times to recruitment solutions for the businesses and life changing career decisions for the students" (Leggott, this volume, p. 30). In this day and age, it is crucial for universities to embed employer engagement in the curriculum and beyond, and Leggott shares some interesting suggestions and examples. **Organ**'s paper offers some very valuable information on the benefits of work placements for the development of modern languages students in terms of experiential and intercultural learning. It also proposes a viable path towards helping languages students gain a better understanding of their employability potential through reflective practice.

3.2.   Developing students' intercultural competence

Papers assembled under the second heading offer ways in which this crucial skill, which is extremely valued by employers, can be fostered and embedded into Modern Foreign Language (MFL) undergraduate programmes.

Guadamillas-Gómez demonstrates how students can improve their language and intercultural competence through participation in virtual exchange schemes. She showcases a telecollaboration project involving universities in Spain and the UK and highlights the professional skill benefits obtained by students taking part. **Parks** presents some of her research, conducted both in UK and US universities, on the link between content modules and the development of Intercultural Competence (IC) and criticality. Content modules, like literature, for example, foster a deeper understanding, awareness and knowledge of the language and culture at hand. Being able to study, compare and discuss the historical and political background in context, as well as linguistic styles and the use of language and metaphors, etc., will instill and cement deep translingual and transcultural competence, which is something highly valued by many employers. **López-Rocha and Vailes** share good practice and reflect on the importance of the promotion and development of Intercultural Communicative Competence (ICC), especially among students about to go on their year abroad; "[t]his paper explores the content and perceived outcomes of a programme aimed at fostering the development of ICC prior to and during the Year Abroad" (López-Rocha & Vailes, this volume, pp. 67-68). López-Rocha and Vailes (this volume) purport that "a programme of this nature is necessary to foster skills involved in the promotion of intercultural citizenship" (p. 68), to ensure that the year abroad is a successful and meaningful experience – an experience of a lifetime that can certainly change and/or shape your whole life.

3.3.   Fostering employability in the classroom

The third section of this volume zooms in on innovative teaching and assessment practices designed to help students become more clearly aware of the transferable skills they are acquiring. In their paper, **Lagares and Reisenleutner** discuss the benefits of rotating poster presentations in boosting students' cognitive skills, motivation and engagement. **Federici**'s contribution reports on the transformative impact of enquiry-based learning approaches on the self-perception of MFL students through the development of critical and analytical skills. **Campbell** explains the reasoning behind the new model of assessment for the Institution-Wide Language Programme (IWLP) at the University of Leeds. As she points out in the abstract, "assessment is a critical part of teaching and learning so it is important that students are encouraged to engage positively with it" (Campbell, this volume, p. 97). It is essential to keep up with the times to develop modern, meaningful, motivating and inclusive assessment that students will be able to share with prospective employees to showcase both their academic and digital skills. In their paper, **Almeida and Puig** make the case for literature teaching in enhancing students' employability skills. Drawing on extensive research findings, they underline the practical benefits of including literature in the languages curriculum. They also report on the development of an innovative project and the website, *Litinclass* which is aimed at expanding the teaching of literature and sharing good practices.

3.4.   Enhancing employability through digital tools

Finally, the fourth section of this volume showcases examples of innovative projects using online collaborative means to support learning and foster a wide range of transferable skills. In her contribution, **Plutino** reports on the TwitTIAMO project which makes creative use of Twitter by encouraging students of Italian to engage in collaborative learning outside of the traditional classroom environment. **Escobar and Krauß** discuss the benefits of online blended learning approaches delivered via the Rosetta Stone® Advantage platform, and provide concrete evidence of a positive impact on the learners' cognitive and organisational skills. **Deacon, Parkin, and Schneider** discuss their experience designing and implementing a new 'Professional French' module in which they wanted to ensure that students not only use and learn French, but also practise and develop digital literacy and competencies. Throughout the module, students will develop a digital portfolio which includes a blog and other digital media, such as videos and voice recordings, that they will be able to share with prospective employers.

4.   Conclusion

The contributions in this collection showcase a series of inventive projects and initiatives accompanied by evidence-based, practical guidance which we hope will enthuse and support classroom practitioners in the higher education languages sector as they seek to integrate employability more firmly into the curriculum. These papers also complement the Corradini, Borthwick, and Gallagher-Brett (2016) volume on *Languages for employability: a handbook*, and are particularly timely in the light of the changing policy environment and the introduction of the Teaching Excellence Framework. The modern languages community undoubtedly faces challenges ahead as the UK appears to be adopting a more inward-looking focus and we are therefore greatly encouraged by the dynamic and outward-facing nature of the teaching practice described so vividly here.

To conclude, we would like to express our gratitude to all the contributors for their excellent work and their help in reviewing the manuscripts thoroughly, as well as all the presenters and delegates who attended InnoConf16 (http://innoconf2016.weebly.com/), enriching the field of Modern Language Teaching thanks to their tremendous contributions. We would also like to thank the University of York and the Department of Language and Linguistic Science for organising and hosting the event, and Sanako (Marie O'Sullivan and David Binns) for their sponsorship.

Carmen Álvarez-Mayo, on behalf of the InnoConf16 organising team, would like to thank the University of York Pro-Vice-Chancellor for Learning, Teaching and Students, John Robinson, and Peter Sells, the Head of the Language and Linguistic Science Department until September 2016, for all their support. Very special thanks to her colleague Lorena López; together they organised the conference and saw it through. Thanks to Ruth Ray, and to all students and colleagues who helped on the day and throughout the journey that brought us here. And, Carmen would also like to express her gratitude to Angela Gallagher-Brett and Franck Michel for their collaboration in making this book happen.

Last but not least, we owe an immense debt of gratitude to Karine Fenix and Sylvie Thouësny at Research-publishing.net for painstakingly guiding us through every step of this volume's publishing process. Their professionalism, dedication and infinite patience are to be commended, and we thank them for their outstanding support.

References

Álvarez-Mayo, C. (2016). 360° employability skills: understanding, cultivating and applying professional and continual development skills [Online]. *York Learning & Teaching Forum.* https://yorkforum.org/2016/11/23/360-employability-skills-understanding-cultivating-and-applying-professional-and-continual-development-skills/

Campbell, C. (2017). Using assessment to showcase employability in IWLP. In C. Álvarez-Mayo, A. Gallagher-Brett & F. Michel (Eds), *Innovative language teaching and learning at university: enhancing employability* (pp. 97-104). Research-publishing.net. https://doi.org/10.14705/rpnet.2017.innoconf2016.659

Chertkovskaya, E., Watt, P., Tramer, S., & Spoelstra, S. (2013). Giving notice to employability. Ephemera: theory & politics in organization. *Ephemera, 13*(4). http://www.ephemerajournal.org/sites/default/files/pdfs/issue/13-4ephemera-nov13.pdf

Corradini, E., Borthwick, K., & Gallagher-Brett, A. (Eds). (2016). *Employability for languages: a handbook.* Research-publishing.net. https://doi.org/10.14705/rpnet.2016.cbg2016.9781908416384

Goria, C., Speicher, O., & Stollhans, S. (Eds). (2016). *Innovative language teaching and learning at university: enhancing participation and collaboration.* Research-publishing.net. https://doi.org/10.14705/rpnet.2016.9781908416322

Leggott, D. (2017). "I'm just a linguist – all I can do is teach or translate". Broadening language graduates' horizons through employer engagement. In C. Álvarez-Mayo, A. Gallagher-Brett & F. Michel (Eds), *Innovative language teaching and learning at university: enhancing employability* (pp. 29-36). Research-publishing.net. https://doi.org/10.14705/rpnet.2017.innoconf2016.652

López-Rocha, S., & Vailes, F. (2017). Developing intercultural communicative competence for the Year Abroad experience. In C. Álvarez-Mayo, A. Gallagher-Brett & F. Michel (Eds), *Innovative language teaching and learning at university: enhancing employability* (pp. 67-75). Research-publishing.net. https://doi.org/10.14705/rpnet.2017.innoconf2016.656

Wyburd, J. (2017). Transnational graduates and employability: challenges for HE language departments. In C. Álvarez-Mayo, A. Gallagher-Brett & F. Michel (Eds), *Innovative language teaching and learning at university: enhancing employability* (pp. 11-19). Research-publishing.net. https://doi.org/10.14705/rpnet.2017.innoconf2016.650

Section 1.

Mapping the 'Global Graduate' landscape

2 Transnational graduates and employability: challenges for HE language departments

Jocelyn Wyburd[1]

Abstract

Drawing on the research done for the British Academy's Born Global project, this chapter explores employer demand for the skills graduates in and with languages can develop. The research outcomes raise challenges for Higher Education (HE) professionals to articulate more clearly the nature of language degrees and the transnational profile of their graduates. Departments need to help students to recognise their employment-related skillset and to understand how to communicate this to prospective employers. The chapter includes practical suggestions and a focus on specific terminology which are recommended to colleagues across the sector.

Keywords: transnational, intercultural, cultural agility.

1. Defining the challenges

In 2016, the British Academy published the data from its Born Global research project on language skills for employability, trade and business (British Academy, 2016a). The project followed concern reflected in national surveys such as Confederation of British Industry (CBI, 2016) annual skills surveys and British Chambers of Commerce reports about the lack of language and intercultural skills amongst current and prospective employees.

1. University of Cambridge, Cambridge, United Kingdom; jmw234@cam.ac.uk

How to cite this chapter: Wyburd, J. (2017). Transnational graduates and employability: challenges for HE language departments. In C. Álvarez-Mayo, A. Gallagher-Brett, & F. Michel (Eds), *Innovative language teaching and learning at university: enhancing employability* (pp. 11-19). Research-publishing.net. https://doi.org/10.14705/rpnet.2017.innoconf2016.650

© 2017 Jocelyn Wyburd (CC BY)

Amongst the data are findings from the small to medium sized enterprises, reported separately for companies who do and do not currently use languages in their business. 67% of those using languages agreed that "foreign language skills are equally as important as sciences, technology, engineering and maths" (Morris & Kashefpakdel, 2014, p. 60) in relation to job prospects for the current and next generation. More importantly, 41% of those respondents who do not use languages also agreed, while only 33% disagreed. Meanwhile 70% of those who use languages and 68% of those who do not, agreed that "multilingual international graduates have a strong advantage in the jobs market" (Morris & Kashefpakdel, 2014, p. 37).

As part of the Born Global research, a large data set was also analysed to explore correlations between language qualifications and three indicators of subsequent labour market success: earnings, employment outcomes, and job satisfaction. The data came from the British Cohort Study of 17,000 people born in England, Scotland and Wales in the same week in 1970. An analysis of the data from the year 2000 (the only year for which it was available) revealed that:

> "Little evidence was found of any direct association between the possession of language qualifications and labour market outcomes at the age of 29, whether measured through earnings, employment outcomes or job satisfaction [...]. While there was some incidence of UK-educated linguists securing superior labour market outcomes, these effects disappeared when statistical controls for social background and academic ability were introduced; this suggests that this association was linked to other factors such as social background rather than language study" (Morris, Kashefpakdel, & Mann, 2014, p. 2).

Thus, on the one hand language graduates should have a massive advantage in the labour market, and on the other hand, from studying a previous generation, those advantages do not appear to be evidenced. This is further borne out by recent data showing unemployment rates six months after graduating – Destinations of Leavers from Higher Education (DLHE) – with caveats about reliability from self-reporting, and the single snapshot in time (HESA, 2013-14). However, as this data forms part of the Key Information Sets published to prospective students, it cannot be ignored (Table 1).

Table 1.   DLHE rate of unemployment of 2013-14 graduates six months after graduation (HESA, 2013-14)

Degree subject	Unemployed
All subjects	6.50%
All Arts, Humanities, Social Sciences	5.60%
Sciences total	6.00%
Languages	6.70%
Business & Administration	7.80%
Computer Science	11.30%
Engineering & Technology	7.70%

It is encouraging that language graduates outperform several more ostensibly vocational subjects, although they slightly underperform the arts, humanities and social sciences as a whole. If they have skillsets that should put them at an advantage, this presents a challenge, requiring a focus on two stakeholder groups: employers and students of language degrees.

2.   Communicating to employers

There is ample evidence, including from Born Global, that the recruitment of transnational, globally agile graduates is not a challenge for employers: they can hire them from outside the UK if, as CBI Skills surveys suggest (CBI, 2016, p. 49), they are dissatisfied with UK graduates[2]. Ironically, it has been noted in the Born Global research how rarely employers specify a requirement for language skills in their graduate recruitment documentation (e.g. British Academy, 2014a, p. 5).

In fact, employers may not fully understand what a language degree involves (British Academy, 2016b). The lead researcher reported in 2015 to the All Party Parliamentary Group on Languages that some expect a language degree

2. This situation may change in the light of Brexit if EU workforce mobility is restricted – which might drive employer pressure on the government for increased language and intercultural training in all education sectors.

to produce employment-specific language skills, and if these are not explicitly evidenced, are thus disappointed. In the process, they may overlook the wider graduate skillset:

> "Language degrees also provide skills well beyond technical proficiency with languages which are important to employers and which can be under-appreciated both by students and by employers" (British Academy, 2016b, p11).

To address this gap in understanding, Born Global challenges the HE sector to define Modern Languages degrees more clearly. Such definitions already exist in the Quality Assurance Agency (QAA) subject benchmark statement (my emphasis):

> "The study of languages enables students to **understand the similarities and differences between cultures.** [...] In this sense it is **inherently intercultural**. The study of languages enables students to **understand ideas and events that cross national boundaries**, the **current and historical relationships between countries**, and the **ways in which other countries interact with the UK**. In this sense it is **transnational**" (QAA, 2015, p. 8).

The benchmark statement further defines language graduates (my emphasis) as follows:

> "The study of a language enables students to **participate in societies whose language they study** and to **operate within different linguistic and cultural contexts**. This places them **in a privileged position** in that they can **reflect on their own society from new perspectives**, thus **increasing their understanding of the concept of citizenship**. They can **compare and contrast diverse visions of the world**, thereby **promoting intercultural understanding** and bringing distinctive **benefits** both **to their own society**, for example, in employment terms, and **to the societies of target languages**" (QAA, 2015, p. 9).

The adoption of this kind of terminology by HE Institutions in prospectuses, on websites and in degree transcripts could assist employers in understanding the skillset of language graduates better. The massively diverse HE context presents further challenges, however; how can employers understand the range of major-minor combinations of subjects or CVs which include language learning through institution wide language programmes (whether for credit or extra-curricular)? Effectively, the sector is producing both graduates *in* languages and graduates *with* languages. In addition to reflecting the benchmark statement descriptors, it is crucial to ensure that language learning outcomes are mapped to the Common European Framework of Reference (Council of Europe, 2001) so that employers also have a transparent account of the language competence of applicants.

3.   Communicating to students

As alluded to above, "given the high-level skills provided by language degree study it is probable that language graduates are under-selling themselves" (British Academy, 2016b, pp. 12-13).

HE language departments have a duty to ensure that their students understand what employers are looking for in order to best demonstrate their unique attributes. The principal researcher for Born Global provided the following insight into employer thinking (my emphasis):

> "Executive directors of global talent use a **complex matrix of skills** to select a successful recruit. They prioritise sector or industry-specific knowledge and a **range of transversal and soft skills. Cultural agility** is an **essential attribute of the global graduate,** as they will be expected to work in multilingual and culturally diverse teams face-to-face and virtually. The ability to **approach a problem from multiple perspectives** and to **take into account different cultural expectations** in finding solutions is key to **effective transnational cooperation**" (Holmes, 2015, p. 9).

This maps well onto the subject benchmark statement above, even though languages are not specifically mentioned. Holmes continues to define the transnational graduate as a 'value-added recruit', who is not necessarily a linguist, but is likely to have been mobile during their studies:

> "The candidate who, in addition to meeting the core requirements of the job specification, can demonstrate an **international outlook** and a **global mind-set**, together with fluency in more than one language and culture, is likely to be selected over the candidate with few or no language skills, whose only experience outside the UK was on holiday" (Holmes, 2015, p. 9).

In the context of the UK National Outward Mobility Strategy, *Gone International* (Bøe & Hurley, 2015) reported on the 2012/13 graduating cohort six months after graduation:

- Mobile graduates were less likely to be unemployed (5.4% vs 6.7%).

- Mobile graduates were more likely to be working abroad (11% vs 2%).

- On average mobile graduates earned more.

- A higher percentage of mobile graduates than non-mobile graduates entered the following sectors: *Professional, Scientific and Technical*, *Education* and *Finance and Insurance*.

As outward mobility is compulsory in language degrees, this data further underpins the language graduate's employability advantage which departments can exploit in their documentation.

To assist students further, departments could download and adapt the language graduate skills grid (Wyburd, 2011) developed within the UCML Shaping the Future project. It suggests five categories of linguistic, cultural and intercultural, intellectual, employment specific, and personal skills, all from which students can select according to their experience and studies.

The importance of this approach is highlighted by reports from both Holmes (2015) and HE Careers Advisors in public symposia, suggesting, for example, that many language graduates fail to highlight their enhanced communication skills in their CVs and application letters. One HE Careers Advisor, at a 2015 London Language Show Symposium on Employability, reported that language students often start by looking for roles explicitly requiring languages (only to be disappointed), or approach employers at careers fairs to ask what 'jobs with languages' they have. As noted above, this is not the way employers work and I believe students need to turn their approach on its head: first seeking careers they are interested in, matching their valuable skillset to these, and then presenting their transnational multilingual credentials within that package rather than putting their languages centre-stage. This approach may challenge their identity as 'linguists', but in employment (as opposed to academia) a 'linguist' refers to the professions of translator, interpreter, teacher or academic, equipped with relevant postgraduate qualifications.

4. Conclusion

With the upcoming HE Teaching Excellence Framework, including metrics related to graduate employment, there is tension about whether it is the role of HE educators to prepare students for employment or deliver more vocational programmes. From the British Academy Born Global evidence (British Academy, 2014a, 2014b, 2016a, 2016b), the transnational skills of the language graduates are already much in demand. There is, however, a major communications challenge for language departments. This involves marketing language degrees to prospective students in terminology which reflects employer demand, in addition to focussing on their intrinsic intellectual content. Furthermore, it puts an onus on language departments and their institutional careers services to educate students to translate the skills gained from their degrees into employer-friendly language and to present themselves to employers as the embodiment of the transnational graduate. As outlined above, I believe the tools and terminology required for these tasks are already in existence and that one major impact from the Born Global research project should be for the sector to adopt these proactively.

References

Bøe, L.,& Hurley, D. (2015). *Gone International.* UK Higher Education International Unit. http://go.international.ac.uk/content/research-and-evidence/go-international-research/gone-international-mobile-students-and-the-0

British Academy. (2014a). *Born Global 02: Small and Medium Enterprises (SMEs) language survey.* http://www.britac.ac.uk/sites/default/files/2.%20SME%20Language%20Survey%20Summary.pdf

British Academy. (2014b). *Born Global 06: British cohort study analysis. Summary and key findings.* http://www.britac.ac.uk/sites/default/files/6.%20British%20Cohort%20Study%20Analysis%20Summary.pdf

British Academy. (2016a). *Born Global. A British Academy project on languages and employability.* http://www.britac.ac.uk/born-global

British Academy. (2016b). *Born Global: implications for higher education.* http://www.britac.ac.uk/sites/default/files/Born%20Global%20-%20Implications%20for%20Higher%20Education.pdf

CBI. (2016). *The right combination: CBI/Pearson education and skills survey 2016.* www.cbi.org.uk/cbi-prod/assets/File/pdf/cbi-education-and-skills-survey2016.pdf

Council of Europe. (2001). *Common European framework of reference for languages: teaching, learning and assessment.* Cambridge: Cambridge University Press.

HESA. (2013-14). *Destinations of leavers from higher education data for the 2013-14 cohort, Table E: Subjects.* https://www.hesa.ac.uk/stats-dlhe

Holmes, B. (2015). Case study: the value-added recruit. In Cambridge Public Policy SRI report, *The value of languages*, (pp. 8-9). http://www.publicpolicy.cam.ac.uk/pdf/value-of-languages

Morris, K., & Kashefpakdel, E. (2014). *Born Global: SME languages survey analysis.* http://www.britac.ac.uk/sites/default/files/2.1%20SME%20Language%20Survey%20Results.pdf

Morris, K., Kashefpakdel, E., & Mann A. (2014). *Are people who speak foreign languages at an advantage in the labour market? An analysis of British Cohort Study data.* http:// www.britac.ac.uk/sites/default/files/6.%20British%20Cohort%20Study%20Analysis%20 Full%20Report.pdf

QAA. (2015). *Subject benchmark statement: languages, cultures and societies.* Quality Assurance Agency. http://www.qaa.ac.uk/publications/information-and-guidance/ publication?PubID=2982#.V0LZfuR-5fY

Wyburd, J. (2011). Skills and attributes of the languages graduate. *Shaping the future: resources for employability.* UCML. http://www.ucml.ac.uk/shapingthefuture/employability

3 The year abroad: understanding the employability skills of the Global Graduate

Cristina López-Moreno[1]

Abstract

This chapter will examine the employability profile of outwardly mobile British graduates and the ways in which their international skillset fits the UK labour market. It will draw upon several recent reports to highlight the current shortage of professionals with such global skills. In this context, the chapter will demonstrate that internationally mobile British graduates can help meet this skill gap and that they are ideally suited to working in the current, increasingly-globalised UK economy. The chapter will also highlight the importance of describing the global skillset in a manner that conveys its value and uniqueness to employers effectively. Drawing upon the author's experience managing international work placements at Sheffield Business School (SBS), it will be argued that many final year students and recent graduates fail to recognise the distinctiveness of their profiles. As job seekers, they typically define themselves through their language skills, whereas the enhanced competencies gained through the year abroad are often not understood or articulated appropriately. Therefore, the importance of a sharp focus on the global skills to reflect the higher demand for such attributes in the UK will be discussed.

Keywords: global graduate, employability, languages, year abroad, mobility.

1. Sheffield Hallam University, Sheffield, United Kingdom; C.L.Moreno@shu.ac.uk

How to cite this chapter: López-Moreno, C. (2017). The year abroad: understanding the employability skills of the Global Graduate. In C. Álvarez-Mayo, A. Gallagher-Brett, & F. Michel (Eds), *Innovative language teaching and learning at university: enhancing employability* (pp. 21-28). Research-publishing.net. https://doi.org/10.14705/rpnet.2017.innoconf2016.651

© 2017 Cristina López-Moreno (CC BY)

1.   Introduction

One of the most prevalent trends in the higher education sector in the UK is its push towards integrating employability in undergraduate courses (Higher Education Academy, 2014a). This principle will only become increasingly significant in future years, particularly in the light of the forthcoming Teaching Excellence Framework (TEF) and its employment metrics (Department for Business and Skills, 2016, p. 21). Many universities, therefore, are seeking to forge closer collaboration with employers and to gain better awareness of their recruiting needs.

According to numerous studies (British Academy, 2016; Diamond et al., 2011; Higher Education Academy, 2014b), the current, highly-globalised UK economy has fostered the need for an internationally-minded workforce. Intercultural professional competencies, as well as foreign language skills, are seen as important requirements to perform effectively in this context. This global skillset is rare amongst UK graduates (British Council, 2013), and increasingly, British employers find themselves looking overseas for the well-qualified, multilingual, globally-minded international graduates they cannot easily find at home.

In this chapter, I will argue that the UK can help bridge this skill gap by encouraging student outward mobility. I will bring in my extensive experience managing international work placements at SBS to illustrate how language graduates who have benefitted from international mobility fit this sought-after profile closely. Our applied language courses are combined honours in Languages with International Business, Tourism or Teaching English to Speakers of Other Languages (TESOL). All our degrees have an embedded 18-month compulsory mobility period abroad; this is split between a study semester at a European university and a work placement year in the target language country. By the time our students graduate they have achieved highly developed cross-cultural competencies and other key core skills. In addition, they have consolidated their subject knowledge and have acquired extensive international work experience. However, despite this well-rounded, multi-faceted profile, our graduates often fail to articulate their professional profiles appropriately. Following the trend observed in language graduates across the UK, they define themselves primarily through their language competencies, and this narrow focus on language skills to the detriment of other core competencies has been proven to limit these graduates' employment avenues (British Academy, 2016). In this chapter, I will argue that understanding and appropriately articulating the full skillset is crucial in allowing linguists and other internationally mobile British graduates to reach their professional potential.

2. The Global Graduate concept

Employers and higher education institutions use the Global Graduate concept to describe a globally-minded young professional with sound intercultural awareness and with the ability to interact effectively in an international environment. Global Graduates are so sought after because they have the usual professional attributes traditionally expected by employers, and *in addition*, the global attributes needed to engage with others and to work effectively in an international professional context (Diamond et al., 2011). Table 1 below shows how both sets of competencies compare.

Table 1.   Core competencies and global competencies comparison

CORE COMPETENCIES Prospects (2015)	GLOBAL COMPETENCIES (Global Graduates into Global Leaders. Diamond et al., 2011 p. 8)

• Good communication
 	
• Effective leadership
 	
• Planning and research
 	
• Teamwork and interpersonal skills
 	
• Self-management
 	
• Relevant work experience
	• Work collaboratively with
	  international teams
	
	• Enhanced communication skills
	
	• Drive and resilience
	
	• Embracing multiple perspectives
	  and challenge thinking

It is worth highlighting that, contrary to what one would expect, multilingualism does not feature prominently in the global skill set. There is conflicting research on this matter, with some reports highlighting the importance of foreign language fluency to UK business (British Academy, 2014, 2016; British Council, 2013; Confederation of British Industry, 2015), and others suggesting that languages are useful but are not a must for most recruiters (e.g. Diamond et al., 2011). The overall consensus seems to be that *languages add value when they are offered in addition to the global skillset*. In other words, multilingualism on its own is less likely to attract recruiters' interest, as the ability to speak another language is rarely the main skill employers look for. The soft-skills associated with language learning and reinforced through the year abroad are, therefore, as or more important to employers than foreign language fluency. This is why it is so crucial for language graduates to, first, recognise their whole set of skills, and second, learn to describe them appropriately.

3.   The year abroad as a differentiating factor

A year of study or working abroad is one of the most reliable paths to global competencies (British Academy, 2012). At SBS, our combined language students develop their global attributes by working overseas in roles which tie in with their degree specialisms. As an example, an International Business with Spanish student may work as a Corporate Purchase Intern for a multinational firm based in Madrid. This combination of experiential, hands-on learning, the immersion in a foreign culture and the need to overcome challenges on a regular basis provide the right ingredients to develop a highly-skilled and much sought-after professional profile.

Global professionals, such as the ones graduating from SBS, find themselves able to gain employment more quickly and have better long-term prospects than graduates without international experience. The findings of the 2014 Erasmus Impact report (European Commission, 2014) confirm this: 64% of international recruiters consider an extended period of residence abroad as important; "internationally mobile students are half as likely to experience long-term unemployment" (ICEF Monitor, 2014, n.p.); one in three students who have undertaken a work placement abroad have been offered a permanent job by their host company. Not only that, but in addition to being better positioned for their first role, Global Graduates can expect a faster progress up the career ladder – particularly if their year abroad has been done as a work placement.

> "Experience of working overseas and immersion in a different culture can catapult a graduate into being considered for rewarding and challenging roles" (Diamond et al., 2011, p. 4).

Despite all the evidence highlighting the enhanced employability prospects for graduates with a year abroad, only a very small minority of British students choose to take part in international mobility programmes. The UK ranks 25th in the world for external mobility in higher education according to the Higher Education Funding Council for England (HEFCE, 2013). The outward mobility ratio for tertiary students in the UK is 1.2%, which contrasts starkly with the 4.3% ratio in Germany (UNESCO Institute of Statistics, 2016). British universities often pride themselves on their internationalisation efforts; however, the vast majority of their investment is focused on inward student recruitment.

The contrast between outward and inward internationalisation trends in UK universities could not be more glaring. A few facts illustrate this matter very clearly. The UK has one of the most internationally diverse student populations in the world, with one student in six being from a foreign country. It is the second country in the world, after the US, which attracts the most overseas students (Universities UK, 2016). The UK hosted 428,724 foreign students in 2016; however, it only sent 27,337 students abroad on either study or work placements – and many of these students lived in English-speaking countries. British universities do not invest in outward mobility sufficiently (HEFCE, 2013) and this is what has created the current global skill gap in the UK labour market. The poor outward mobility ratio is seen as a weakness in the British higher education sector, a fact reflected in HEFCE's (2013) UK Strategy for

Outward Mobility, with its vision of increasing the number of internationally mobile British students by 2020.

4.   Conclusions

In order to maximise their career opportunities, graduates with a year abroad need to appreciate that they are value-added professionals and that their international experience is their unique selling point. They must also learn to define their skills in employer-friendly language, utilising vocabulary that is familiar to recruiters. At SBS, final year language students are encouraged to brand themselves as Global Graduates and use skill mapping exercises to gain awareness of their attributes. They also learn to define their profile in employer-friendly language. To this effect, the following terminology is useful:

- Linguists must define themselves as **Global Graduates** with extended experience of studying and/or working abroad.

- Linguists must emphasise their **global mindset**; that is, their cultural agility, maximum adaptability and their ability to build a quick rapport with professionals of other nationalities. Demonstrating these attributes with examples taken from the year abroad will reinforce their global label even further.

- Linguists must also highlight their **global skillset** and draw employers' attention to their extended experience of working collaboratively in multicultural teams, their resilience and problem-solving abilities and indeed, their foreign language and subject-specific skills.

Internationally, mobile graduates are highly-skilled individuals. The challenge they face lies not with their profile, but with their ability to showcase their unique set of attributes. If they can do so successfully, they will be in the best possible position to realise their professional potential.

References

British Academy. (2012). *Valuing the year abroad.* http://www.ucml.ac.uk/sites/default/files/pages/160/Valuing%20the%20Year%20Abroad.pdf

British Academy. (2014). *Prospering wisely: how the humanities and social sciences enrich our lives.* http://www.britac.ac.uk/prosperingwisely/

British Academy. (2016). *Born global: implications for higher education.* http://www.britac.ac.uk/sites/default/files/Born%20Global%20-%20Implications%20for%20Higher%20Education_1.pdf

British Council. (2013). *Languages for the future.* https://www.britishcouncil.org/sites/default/files/languages-for-the-future-report.pdf

Confederation of British Industry. (2015). *Education and skills survey. Inspiring growth.* http://www.cbi.org.uk/business-issues/people-and-skills/

Department for Business and Skills. (2016). *Teaching excellence framework. Technical consultation for year 2.* https://www.gov.uk/government/uploads/system/uploads/attachment_data/file/523340/bis-16-262-teaching-excellence-framework-techcon.pdf

Diamond, A., Walkley, L., Forges, P., Hughes, T., & Sheen, J. (2011). *Global graduates into global leaders.* http://www.ucml.ac.uk/sites/default/files/shapingthefuture/101/CIHE%20-%201111GlobalGradsFull.pdf

European Commission. (2014). *Erasmus impact study.* http://ec.europa.eu/education/library/study/2014/erasmus-impact_en.pdf

HEFCE. (2013). UK Strategy for outward mobility. *Higher Education Funding Council for England.* http://go.international.ac.uk/sites/default/files/UK%20HE%20International%20Unit%20UK%20Strategy%20for%20Outward%20Mobility%20Version%201.0.pdf

Higher Education Academy. (2014a). *Employability.* https://www.heacademy.ac.uk/services/consultancy/employability

Higher Education Academy. (2014b). *Internationalising higher education framework.* https://www.heacademy.ac.uk/system/files/resources/internationalisingheframeworkfinal.pdf

ICEF Monitor. (2014). New study makes the link between study abroad and employability. *Edu Services.* http://www.studyinchina.com.my/web/page/link-between-study-abroad-and-employability/

Prospects. (2015). *What skills do employers want?* https://www.prospects.ac.uk/careers-advice/applying-for-jobs/what-skills-do-employers-want

UNESCO Institute of Statistics. (2016). *Global flow of tertiary-level students*. http://uis. unesco.org/en/uis-student-flow

Universities UK. (2016). *International higher education in facts and figures*. http:// www.universitiesuk.ac.uk/policy-and-analysis/reports/Pages/international-facts-and-figures-2016.aspx

4 "I'm just a linguist – all I can do is teach or translate". Broadening language graduates' horizons through employer engagement

Dawn Leggott[1]

Abstract

Employers in the UK recognise that a lack of language skills can limit their company's international growth. Many students on language degrees, however, feel unprepared for working in a business environment. The final year 'Working with Languages' module on Leeds Beckett University's language degrees aims to help the students to expand their career horizons beyond teaching and translating through real-world engagement with local employers. This chapter will summarise the implementation and impact of this core module and highlight some extra-curricular employer engagement[2] activities for students on language degrees. Language graduates can bring much more to a small, medium or large international business than they may think. Employer engagement, whether embedded within the curriculum or offered as an extra-curricular option, can help them to realise that they are not 'just a linguist' and can add value through their communication skills and international mind-set.

Keywords: languages, jobs, employability, employer engagement, work-related learning, authentic project.

1. Dawn Leggott Consulting Ltd, Leeds, United Kingdom; dawn@dawnleggott.co.uk

2. The author will willingly discuss the incorporation of employer engagement within or beyond the language degree curriculum in further detail with individual universities; www.dawnleggott.co.uk.

How to cite this chapter: Leggott, D. (2017). "I'm just a linguist – all I can do is teach or translate". Broadening language graduates' horizons through employer engagement. In C. Álvarez-Mayo, A. Gallagher-Brett, & F. Michel (Eds), *Innovative language teaching and learning at university: enhancing employability* (pp. 29-36). Research-publishing.net. https://doi.org/10.14705/rpnet.2017.innoconf2016.652

© 2017 Dawn Leggott (CC BY)

1. Introduction

Ask anyone, including some students on language degrees, what jobs you can do with languages, and the first two answers they may give are teaching or translation. Both of these career paths are valid for linguists, but should be selected as a career choice rather than through a lack of awareness of other options. Universities can broaden language students' horizons through the involvement of local small and medium-sized employers, either within or beyond the curriculum.

This chapter presents some practical ways in which businesses and students of languages can collaborate for mutual benefit, leading at times to recruitment solutions for the businesses and life changing career decisions for the students.

2. What do employers want?

Recent reports show that 45% of businesses recognise foreign language skills as beneficial to them (Confederation of British Industry/Pearson, 2015) and that the UK loses out almost GBP50 billion a year in international business opportunities due to poor language skills in the workforce (All Party Parliamentary Group on Modern Languages, 2014).

Graduates with language skills, particularly graduates with language degrees, possess many of the skills required in today's global economy. Employers' job descriptions may not specifically state a language requirement, but language graduates should not underestimate the value they can add to companies. They possess cultural agility, an ability to approach a situation from multiple perspectives, as well as intercultural, global and communicative skills as a result of living abroad and integrating into another culture (British Academy, 2016; Holmes, 2016).

At an employer forum run twice a year to enable contacts at local Small and Medium-sized Enterprises (SMEs) to feed into the language degree curriculum and related extra-curricular activities at Leeds Beckett University, the employers were unequivocal in their views on how universities might best prepare their language degree students for a business environment: "Get students out to businesses and get businesses into universities".

3. Getting students out to businesses and businesses into universities

Employer engagement with university students of languages can either be embedded within the curriculum or offered as an extra-curricular activity.

3.1. Embedding employer engagement within the curriculum

One way to show students how they can use their languages in a context other than education or translation is to require them to do so and to assess them on the outcomes.

One example of this is the award-winning[3] 'Working with Languages' module for all final year students on any language degree at Leeds Beckett University for which I was the module leader. Using their language skills to find relevant information which is not as easily accessible to the employers due to their lack of language competence, their intercultural and communication skills, as well as their access to a wealth of market data and other resources through the University's library, the students carried out an authentic market research project in small teams to help a local company (usually an SME) to move into a new export market. Each project brief was written by the company according to guidelines provided by the module leader to ensure parity of task and workload across the different briefs. During a one-off visit to the company, the students gained a deeper understanding of the project brief and useful information about the company's product or service. They were also able to clarify any queries throughout the project with a named contact at the company (typically

3. UK Trade and Investment Languages for Export award.

a marketing manager). The companies ranged from small businesses with less than 50 employees up to larger organisations with around 700 employees and a turnover of about GBP100 million per business year. The module ran throughout the academic year and consisted of seminars, team tutorials and an innovative Employer Day. More interactive than a graduate fair, the Employer Day was more like a 'speed-dating' event in which the students made professional, rather than personal, contacts. This gave the students valuable experience of interacting in small groups with business people who value language skills and with alumni from their degree programme. Indeed, this networking event had, at times, a direct effect on the initial career decisions which students made upon graduation. For example:

> "[…] guest speakers […] held interactive sessions detailing their own experiences and how they had achieved success […]. The most useful of these sessions was the 'Employer Day' […] to broaden our connections amongst several different industries, but also to give us confidence in our employability after university" (Laura Biswas, Regional Sales Executive, LinkedIn recommendation, 2015[4]).

At the end of the module, the students presented their findings to the company in the form of a professional presentation and written business report. They were also required to write an assessed individual reflection in order to make more explicit the relevance of this experience for their forthcoming job search (Kolb, 1984; Rich, 2015). The students' reflections and the annual feedback from the employers showed that this was a win-win situation for both the employers and the vast majority of the students. The employers got to know a pool of soon-to-be graduates with language skills and, crucially, an international mind-set, who could help their company meet its export and other international goals (Leslie Silver International Faculty, 2010). Almost all of the employers worked with different cohorts of students on the module over successive years, providing project briefs for different export markets. The students commented in their individual reflections, through direct, informal communication with the module

---

4. www.linkedin.com/in/dawnleggott

leader and in the individual written feedback on the Employer Day that they had expanded their international business communication skills, commercial awareness, confidence, connections and ultimately their career horizons. For example:

> "I will be starting a new job as an International Sales Coordinator [...]. I wouldn't have got the job without the way your module helped me to sell myself and showcase how transferable my skills are in different job roles" (Sarah Cottingham, LinkedIn message, May 2016).

Employer engagement should not, however, only be incorporated into the curriculum in the language students' final year of study. In today's competitive graduate employment market, making the transition from a student to a professional mind-set and gaining relevant experience to make themselves work-ready cannot start just in Level 6 (their final year of study). It is beyond the scope of this chapter to detail ways in which employer engagement can be incorporated into the curriculum from the students' first year of study and it will depend upon each university's context, but some examples can be found in Corradini, Borthwick, and Gallagher-Brett (2016).

3.2. Employer engagement beyond the curriculum

The embedding of employer engagement into the language degree curriculum may not be feasible in all university contexts. The following extra-curricular opportunities can be tailored specifically to the context of students on language degrees:

- *Mentoring* – local employers working in international business or language degree alumni act as face-to-face or email mentors for final year students.

- *Work Shadowing* – one-day work shadowing of language degree alumni or local export employers to gain experience of professional contexts where the students' skill sets can add value.

- *Work Experience* – a short (one or two week) unpaid placement or a longer paid internship organised, for example, through the University Placement Office or Careers Service. Students can often gain more varied work experience in an SME than on a large company's internship scheme, as they often work in roles across the whole company and the tasks can be tailored to fit the strengths and interests of each individual.

- *Assessment and Selection workshops* – these interactive experiences, such as those run by Smart Resourcing Solutions (2016), allow students to practise the typical processes used by graduate recruiters.

- *Graduate workshops and resources* – the GradStart programme (Akonia, 2016) is designed for recent graduates who are either still unsure about their career preferences after graduation or have started a graduate job in an SME which is too small to run a graduate scheme. Students and recent graduates can also benefit from the extensive online resources and workshops on the Learning to Leap website (Shindler, n.d.).

- *Language degree alumni* – alumni are invaluable members of a university's employer forum, mentors to current students, guest speakers and providers of work opportunities. Social media, particularly LinkedIn, can be an effective way of keeping in touch with alumni, and current students can use LinkedIn to see what jobs alumni from their degree have done and especially their career trajectory, rather than just their first job upon graduation. Social media can also be used to connect students, alumni and employers who value language skills, and to share relevant job opportunities.

- Most of the above extra-curricular, non-assessed activities can be incorporated into a *University Employability Award* so that they are officially recorded and recognised.

4.   Conclusion

In order to make a successful transition from university life to professional life, undergraduates need to be aware of employers' requirements and needs, and how the skills they have developed through their language learning add value to businesses (Leggott & Stapleford, 2007). Getting students out to businesses and businesses into universities can help to ensure that graduates with language skills consider all the options open to them, so that if they do ultimately choose to work in teaching or translating, this is due to career choice and not to a lack of imagination. In this way, no language student by the end of their course should feel that, "I'm just a linguist. All I can do is teach or translate".

References

Akonia. (2016). *GradStart – essential business skills for young employees.* http://www.akonia.com/GradStart

All Party Parliamentary Group on Modern Languages. (2014). *APPG launches manifesto for languages.* https://www.britishcouncil.org/education/schools/support-for-languages/thought-leadership/appg/news/manifesto-for-languages

British Academy. (2016). *Born global: implications for higher education.* http://www.britac.ac.uk/news/british-academy-publishes-evidence-born-global

Confederation of British Industry/Pearson. (2015). *Skills emergency could 'starve growth' - CBI/Pearson survey.* http://www.cbi.org.uk/news/skills-emergency-could-starve-growth-cbi-pearson-survey/

Corradini, E., Borthwick, K., & Gallagher-Brett, A. (Eds). (2016). *Employability for languages: a handbook.* Dublin Ireland: Research-publishing.net. https://doi.org/10.14705/rpnet.2016.cbg2016.9781908416384

Holmes, B. (2016). *The value of languages.* Cambridge: the Cambridge public policy strategic research initiative. http://www.publicpolicy.cam.ac.uk/pdf/value-of-languages

Kolb, D. A. (1984). *Experiential learning: experience as the source of learning and development.* Englewood Cliffs: Prentice-Hall.

Leggott, D., & Stapleford, J. (2007). Internationalisation and employability. In E. Jones & S. Brown (Eds), *Internationalising higher education* (pp. 120-134). London: Routledge.

Leslie Silver International Faculty. (2010). *Ian Burn, Camira Fabrics* [video file]. https://www.youtube.com/watch?v=Kxg0KaegtjM

Rich, J. (2015). *Employability: degrees of value.* Oxford: Higher Education Policy Institute.

Shindler, D. (n.d.). *Learning to leap.* www.learningtoleap.co.uk

Smart Resourcing Solutions. (2016). *Assessment and selection workshop.* https://www.smart-resourcing-solutions.com/#!universities/c1bav

5 "Languages in the workplace": embedding employability in the foreign language undergraduate curriculum

Alison Organ[1]

Abstract

This case study examines student perceptions of the experiential value of a work placement carried out as part of a languages degree programme. The data for the case study consists of a corpus of 67 reports submitted from 2011 to 2015, reflecting on placements carried out in Europe, Japan, the UK and the US. The data offers a student view of the impact of the placement on their linguistic prowess, character development, employability and career plans. The case study compares these with the soft skills increasingly required in employment, and concludes that the reflective nature of the work placement report is beneficial to students in preparation for marketing themselves to potential employers.

Keywords: languages, work placement, employability, key skills, study abroad.

1.   Background

Students at York St John University are required to carry out a 15-day work placement at some point during their second year. As students on our languages degree programmes spend their second year studying abroad at partner

1. York St John University, York, United Kingdom; a.organ@yorksj.ac.uk

How to cite this chapter: Organ, A. (2017). "Languages in the workplace": embedding employability in the foreign language undergraduate curriculum. In C. Álvarez-Mayo, A. Gallagher-Brett, & F. Michel (Eds), *Innovative language teaching and learning at university: enhancing employability* (pp. 37-45). Research-publishing.net. https://doi.org/10.14705/rpnet.2017.innoconf2016.653

© 2017 Alison Organ (CC BY)

universities, a distance module was created. The students are required to find and negotiate their placement themselves, although guidance is given by the module director. The student completes an agreement form in discussion with the supervisor in the host organisation, who, crucially, also signs a completion form to confirm that the placement was carried out.

The module is assessed by a 5000-word reflective report detailing the steps taken to arrange the placement, the nature of the host organisation, a discussion of language and communication issues encountered, and evaluations of the student's performance and the impact of the placement on his or her career plans (Organ, 2016).

Students are given complete freedom in their choice of placement. They are encouraged to carry it out abroad, because of the benefits in terms of linguistic progress and personal achievement, although some choose to find placements at home for practical or personal reasons. Students abroad are often employed by their host university to provide English conversation classes, or find placements in the international office. Others are assigned to local schools, or apply to commercial language schools. Those who do not want to teach often find placements in retail, hospitality, or voluntary work.

In the UK, some students look for placements in schools, particularly if they are planning to go into teaching. Others apply to museums or tourist offices. Students of British Sign Language (BSL) approach special schools, local council services, or centres and charities for the Deaf.

2.   Literature review

Work placement modules can be good examples of experiential learning as advocated by Kolb (1984), who drew on earlier work to establish his experiential learning cycle. More recently, authors such as Kohonen (2001), and Phipps and Gonzalez (2004), have researched this practice within the specific field of foreign language learning.

2.1.   Experiential learning

Work placement modules align closely with Kolb's (1984) notion that "Learning is the process whereby knowledge is created through the transformation of experience" (p. 38). Moreover, Kolb's (2014) revised edition of his seminal work "pictures the workplace as a learning environment that can enhance and supplement formal education and can foster personal development through meaningful work and career-development opportunities" (p. 4).

Although Kolb (1984) proposes an experiential learning cycle, the structure of the report submitted by the students in this case study more closely follows Gibbs' (1988) reflective cycle (Figure 1).

Figure 1.   The elements of the placement report, in alignment with Gibbs' (1988) reflective cycle

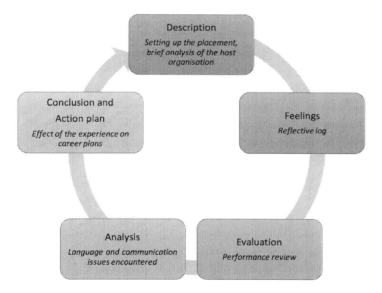

Kohonen (2001) approaches experiential learning from the point of view of language education, arguing that language teaching "has a broader goal than

promoting linguistic and communicative skills only" (p. 2). His claim that it "contributes to the wider task of fostering the students' personal growth" (Kohonen, 2001, p. 2) strikes a chord in the light of the reports which make up this case study.

2.2. Intercultural learning

Phipps and Gonzalez (2004) argue that for language teaching to survive in the current climate, we need to empower students to 'live' the language rather than to just 'have' it.

They offer a concept of 'languaging' as opposed to 'language learning', as shown in Table 1. In their words, this is the process of becoming "active agents in creating their human environment" (Phipps & Gonzalez, 2004, p. 2). In short, "[l]anguaging is a life skill. It is inextricably interwoven with social experience – living in society – and it develops and changes constantly as that experience evolves and changes" (Phipps & Gonzalez, 2004, p. 2).

Table 1.   Extracts from Phipps and Gonzalez (2004, p. 3) concept of 'languaging', adapted from Barnett (1994)

	Language learning	Languaging
Context	Classroom focus	Whole social world
Outcome	Assessed performance	Feel and fluency
Aim	Accuracy and measurable knowledge	Meaning-making and human connection
Disposition	Competition	Open, collective exploration and exchange
Cultures	Learning about	Living in and with
Position	Language at a distance	Language from within
Task	Complex	Supercomplex

Many of these 'languaging' skills, such as 'meaning-making and human connection', and carrying out 'supercomplex' tasks, are developed by students on work placements in their target language context, be it a spoken foreign language or BSL.

3. The case study

The data for this case study consists of a corpus of 67 reports (anonymised and coded with the country and year of writing) submitted from 2011 to 2015, detailing placements carried out in France, Germany, Spain, Japan, the UK and the US. The qualitative data shows that the students value the opportunity to reflect on their experience, and recognise the development of many of the skills mentioned above.

3.1. Advantages of the model

Many students comment on the value of having to secure the placement themselves, and on the importance of the reflective process in helping them to evaluate their experience.

Setting up the placement:
> "What I learnt about myself during my placement is I am proactive and I am able to show initiative by finding a work placement without the assistance of my host university" [SP12/2].

Reflection:
> "The completion of a daily log improved my ability to reflect on the successes and issues of the day and how I reacted to different situations" [FR13/5].

3.2. What do the students learn from the placement?

Many students who carried out their placement in a target language context found that this benefitted their language learning and intercultural understanding, and in some cases their understanding of their other degree subject:

> "I believe that this was an extremely valuable experience for me, equal in value to the entire semester spent abroad" [FR12/1].

Language improvement:

> "It gave me the motivation to study and practice my Japanese language skills in my free time in order to become better at my job. I wrote in my journal after my fourth shift that 'I am disappointed in myself that I can't speak freely to these people" [JP15/4].

Self-confidence:

> "My final shift [...] was a real eye opener. Despite me feeling that I had been the 'awkward English girl', my colleagues and my team leaders had all said to me that I was a pleasure to work with. I was delighted!" [FR13/1].

Application of theory to practice:

> "I was able to acquire invaluable work experience which combined both aspects of my joint honours degree; [...] Intellectually, I was able to take the theoretical side of my academic studies and use the skills in real-life situations" [FR14/5].

3.3. Soft skills

According to the National Careers Service (n.d.), the 'soft skills' employers look for are: communicating, making decisions, showing commitment, flexibility, time management, leadership skills, creativity, problem-solving skills, being a team player, accepting responsibility, and being able to work under pressure.

Being aware of one's own competencies in these areas is a skill in itself, as highlighted by Wyburd (2016), who noted that many languages graduates enter the job market unable to identify to employers the skills that their degree has developed in them. Many of these elements are mentioned in the reports, showing that the reflective process helps the students to recognise the skills they have developed:

> "In terms of occupational skills I have acquired as a result of this placement, I think building my confidence in both languages and in the

workplace environment would be the biggest factors. I feel that this has had a knock-on effect with other skills, such as communication, team-working and leading, organisation, self-management and autonomy within the working environment, and a willingness to learn" [FR15/1].

Communication:

"This placement has honestly been one of the best experiences of my life, this may be because it was abroad but it has given me so much insight into myself and on how to communicate well with others and everyone around me" [JP15/4].

Time management:

"The most useful thing I learned was how to properly organise my time" [GE15/1].

Leadership skills:

"I observed carefully the techniques of the management as I may have to use similar techniques in my future career" [FR13/2].

Teamwork and intercultural understanding:

"This work placement has given me the confidence to consider the possibility of returning to Spain in the future to work as I have proved to myself that I am able to work in a team of people from a foreign country and still be able to complete the tasks required of me without any problems" [SP11/1].

Accepting responsibility:

"By the end of the placement I was given my own set of keys to open/ close the bar while Michael was unavailable and was even given the job of paying the bills" [JP15/4].

Ability to work under pressure:

"Despite all of the language and communication problems which I encountered, I really enjoyed the challenges of working in a foreign environment where each day was a considerably bigger challenge than working in an English supermarket" [FR13/5].

3.4.   Impact on career plans

Many students comment that the experience had a significant effect on their plans for the future, even in cases where the placement itself had not lived up to their expectations:

"It has been an undeniably beneficial experience, even if it was just to clarify that working as a teacher in Japan was something not for me" [JP11/2].

"Overall my experience [...] has forced me to evaluate what I would like to gain from my future studies and, eventually, my career. It has made me more confident not only in communication and a workplace environment but also of my goals, which previously were unfocused and not particularly career driven" [FR13/4].

4.   Conclusion

The findings of this study suggest that students who carry out work placements, particularly in a target language environment, find them valuable in ways which extend beyond their linguistic progress. Alongside the elements mentioned in this report, students comment on the improvement to their oral and aural competence, as well as their understanding of cultural differences. Most report an improvement in their autonomy and professionalism, some discovering reserves of confidence and competence that they were unaware of. While many comment on the fact that the placement clarified their career path, some find that it gave them a renewed appetite for further study.

Finally, the reflection on the experiential learning process gives them an opportunity to articulate the skills they have acquired, which may enable them to present themselves more favourably to potential employers.

References

Barnett, R. (1994). *The Limits of competence: knowledge, higher education and society.* Buckingham: Open University Press.

Gibbs, G. (1988). *Learning by doing: a guide to teaching and learning methods.* Oxford: FEU.

Kohonen, V. (2001). *Experiential learning in foreign language education.* Harlow: Longman.

Kolb, D. A. (1984). *Experiential learning: experience as the source of learning and development* (1st ed.). Englewood Cliffs: Prentice-Hall.

Kolb, D. A. (2014). *Experiential learning: experience as the source of learning and development* (2nd ed.). New Jersey: Pearson.

National Careers Service. (n.d.). *What are the soft skills employers want?* https://nationalcareersservice.direct.gov.uk/aboutus/newsarticles/Pages/Spotlight-SoftSkills.aspx

Organ, A. (2016). Work placements for languages students: a transformative experience. In E. Corradini, K. Borthwick & A. Gallagher-Brett (Eds), *Employability for languages: a handbook* (pp. 25-28). Dublin: Research-publishing.net. http://dx.doi.org/10.14705/rpnet.2016.cbg2016.458

Phipps, A., & Gonzalez, M. (2004). *Modern languages: learning and teaching in an intercultural field.* London: Sage.

Wyburd, J. (2016). *Transnational graduates and employability: challenges for HE colleagues.* Keynote address for the conference Innovative Language Teaching and Learning at University: Enhancing Employability. York.

Section 2.

Developing students' intercultural competence

6 Building global graduates and developing transnational professional skills through a telecollaboration project in foreign language education

Mª Victoria Guadamillas Gómez[1]

Abstract

The development of e-literacies and e-skills is of primary importance in gaining transferable aptitudes for the job market. Students in higher education need to take part in shared intercultural experiences which allow them to understand and cope with their peers in preparation for their futures. Furthermore, virtual exchange of information, development of language skills and interpersonal relationships can allow these future employees to respond better to demands of the job market. This paper describes a case study involving a virtual project developed between the University of Warwick (UK) and the University of Castilla-La Mancha (Spain) aimed at increasing exposure to the foreign language (English/Spanish), and to raise cultural awareness among British and Spanish university students, hence making them more employable in the future.

Keywords: didactic innovation, foreign language learning, intercultural competence, professional skills, oral skills.

1. University of Castilla-La Mancha, Toledo, Spain; Victoria.Guadamillas@uclm.es

How to cite this chapter: Guadamillas Gómez, M. V. (2017). Building global graduates and developing transnational professional skills through a telecollaboration project in foreign language education. In C. Álvarez-Mayo, A. Gallagher-Brett, & F. Michel (Eds), *Innovative language teaching and learning at university: enhancing employability* (pp. 49-58). Research-publishing.net. https://doi.org/10.14705/rpnet.2017.innoconf2016.654

© 2017 Mª Victoria Guadamillas Gómez (CC BY)

1.   Introduction

There is a substantial literature exploring the use of technologies in higher education (O'Dowd, 2005, 2007; Romaña Correa, 2015). In the context of foreign language education, the term telecollaboration has recently emerged as an:

> "Internet-based intercultural exchange between people of different cultural/national backgrounds, set up in an institutional context with the aim of developing both language skills and intercultural communicative competence […] through structured tasks" (Helm & Guth, 2010, p. 14).

Social media sites such as Facebook, Twitter and Skype provide opportunities for students around the world to take part in conversations with other native speaking students. These conversational exchanges allow learners to practise the target language in real contexts by increasing the time of exposure significantly, and thus allowing for a greater understanding of other related aspects of the target language and culture that might be useful and transferable to their personal and professional skills set.

In the field of second and foreign language teaching, many projects have described how online intercultural exchanges support language practice – speaking and listening skills – and cultural awareness (O'Dowd, 2007). According to O'Dowd and Lewis (2016), online intercultural exchanges lead to the development of foreign language and intercultural communication skills, which "students need to be able to gain for employment in a globalised labour market" (p. 7). O'Dowd and Lewis (2016) also refer to e-literacies and e-skills developed through asynchronous tools (such as e-mail) and synchronous ones (such as Skype and videoconferencing), which enhance the ability to communicate clearly and effectively in a foreign language at a distance. Similarly, Romaña Correa (2015, p. 144) describes a study at the Language Institute of the Universidad Distrital Francisco José de Caldas, Bogotá, in which 12 adult learners of English as a Foreign Language (EFL) used Skype to communicate with native speakers elsewhere. Results indicated that learners used the target language as a means of constructing their own social networks, a finding in line with Maynard and Peräkylä's (2003) claim that "it is partly through language that humans 'do' the social world" (p. 233).

In another study, Cunningham and Vyatkina (2012) underline the positive effects of the strategic use of modal verbs for expressing polite requests, as well as a moderate effect on learners' use of the subjunctive mood to establish social distance in exchanges of this kind. The authors note that

> "[t]hese results add further support for the use of intercultural online exchanges mediated by data-driven instruction in the foreign language classroom" (Cunningham & Vyatkina, 2012, p. 422).

These considerations were the starting points for the development of the present project.

2.   The project 'language and culture'

2.1.   Participants and context

One hundred participants were involved in the project, fifty from the Faculty of Education at the University of Castilla-La Mancha (UCLM) and fifty from the Language Centre at Warwick University. The participants at UCLM were in their second year of Early Childhood Education and were taking an EFL course as part of their degree programme in the Faculty of Education. The students from Warwick were in the second or third year of their degree programmes, but were not necessarily studying to become teachers.

The level of proficiency in English or Spanish was not completely homogeneous. Most students at UCLM had an intermediate level of English equivalent to B1 of the Common European Framework of Reference for languages (Council of Europe, 2001). However, four students were below this level, and just two had reached B2. In Warwick, most participants had a B2 level of Spanish. Not all the students in Warwick were native speakers of English, but most had been living in the country for more than ten years and had C1 or C2 levels in English.

Students at UCLM are required to complete the course English II or French II to become Early Childhood or Primary Education teachers. Receptive and productive skills are dealt with on these programmes, as well as aspects related to language teaching. Warwick students study Spanish as an elective language programme at the University's Language Centre. According to records taken from previous tests, students struggle with oral skills at both institutions, which O'Dowd and Lewis (2016) consider vital for employability and which are generally more effective when completing written tasks. Also, whereas most students at Warwick had been involved in virtual projects before, this was not the case with the UCLM cohort.

2.2.　Analysis of needs

The intervention began in September 2015 and was planned as a six-week pilot project, plus a week of reflection. Before designing students' tasks, an analysis of their needs was conducted in both institutions by tutors. Among the needs identified in tests and through observation were:

- lack of fluency in simple oral interventions;

- anxiety, nervousness and lack of confidence in oral tests;

- educational, social and cultural weaknesses;

- lack of vocabulary related to simple intercultural and cross-cultural issues.

After careful analysis, the telecollaborative project 'language and culture' sought to address these weaknesses in order to develop learners' professional communication skills.

In what follows, the preparation, implementation and evaluation of the project are described.

2.3.   Action plan

2.3.1.   Phase I: preparation

During the 2-week preparation process, professors/tutors at both institutions agreed on the exchange time, the type of tasks and communication with students, and the evaluation phases.

At this stage, six topics were shared with students in Warwick through a plan on Blackboard and with UCLM's students using Moodle. Participants at both institutions received a weekly e-mail with the questions for reflection related to the topic. Every task was designed to be developed in a week. The average time of communication was thirty minutes in both English and Spanish. The main aim of giving students defined questions was to provide structured prompts to help overcome shyness and give them a specific starting point for communicating with each other. Tutors also monitored students' involvement through oral or written assignments carried out subsequently in class.

2.3.2.   Phase II: implementation

Regarding online task design, Kurek (2015) notes the need to include specific instructions to decrease geographical and cultural distance and build bridges for intercultural contact. Chapelle (2001) describes some notable characteristics in the process of setting tasks, including the need for tasks to be practical, adaptable and meaningful and to be presented in context. In the current project, particular attention was paid to the tasks. These aimed to reflect students' shared experiences by addressing issues of common interest in their age group, as well as other aspects related to intercultural understanding which might have enhanced their broader skills set and hence improved their future employability. Table 1 shows the different tasks for the first six weeks of the project.

Table 1. Tasks and questions for interaction

Title	Procedure	Questions for reflection
Week 1. First Encounters	Students prepare a presentation about themselves and share it with their virtual exchange partner.	Where do you live? How many languages do you speak? Have you ever been in England or in Spain?
Week 2. My University Life	Students talk about university and their studies. They can focus on their daily activities at university, courses they like, social groups they are involved in or any other aspect related to their studies.	Where is your university? Do you like a subject (discipline in your studies) in particular? Have you ever failed a course at university? Do you take part in any social group at university?
Week 3. Food and Eating	Students share a typical dish or a recipe from their country. They also discuss international food and their favourite food/s and how to prepare them.	Is there a typical dish in your country? What do usually have for dinner or lunch? What time do you have lunch? What dish are you best at cooking?
Week 4. Avoiding Stereotypes	Students discuss how true or false some extended stereotypes are from the cultural reality or society they live in. Students can also discuss if it is important to overcome stereotypes when you study a foreign language.	Is it true that all Spaniards take a siesta every afternoon? Are the Spaniards loud and outgoing? Are the British always punctual and good-mannered?
Week 5. Youth and World Job Market	Students share with their virtual exchange partner aspects related to young people and the job market in their countries.	Do you work? Is it easy to find a job in England/Spain when you finish your studies at University? What job would you like to have in the future? Would it be possible to work in your country?
Week 6. On the news	Students look for a recent news story online either in English or Spanish. Once they have read it, they have to share it with their exchange partner.	Do you think that news includes a lot of violence nowadays? Do you normally listen to the news?
Extra Task. Reflection on my learning	Complete a questionnaire and group work	Would you like to keep talking with your exchange partner?

2.3.3. Phase III: evaluation

Researchers at UCLM and Warwick developed the tools for evaluation. These were an initial pre-project online questionnaire, a mid-project face-to-face semi-structured interview and a post-project final questionnaire.

This section focuses on the final questionnaire, which aimed to analyse the extent of students' regular (weekly) participation in the project and whether they had completed the activities proposed for each of the scheduled exchanges. The questionnaire also enabled students to rate their experience in the project and to respond to the following items on a scale of one to four (none, a little, quite a bit, completely):

- tasks have allowed me to work on fluency and pronunciation in English/ Spanish;

- thanks to this project, I became aware of some intercultural aspects related to either Spanish or British culture;

- conversations through Skype, Whatsapp etc. allowed me to break initial cultural stereotypes;

- I consider that I improved negotiating skills and task completion through peer-work.

The questionnaire also provided an opportunity for open comments.

Figure 1 illustrates the high percentage of students (88.3%) who completed all virtual conversational exchanges, and who did all activities, or more than three (essays or oral expositions following the conversation phase). The number of participants who did not complete the online exchanges was quite low (three students out of 50 participants). These data are for UCLM participants, but similar findings can be extrapolated for participants at Warwick, since they shared tasks with their partners in UCLM.

Figure 1.   Results of participation and task completion (UCLM)

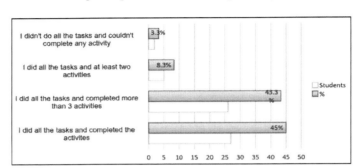

In valuing their experience of the project and responding to the 4 items listed above, 88% of students answered 3 (quite a bit). As for the open comments, some of them indicated the benefits that they observed in relation to their future employability, their intercultural understanding and the increase in their motivation. Thus, a participant from UCLM noted:

"I found [it] really interesting talking about the job market in Britain. They have more possibilities to find a job soon when they finish their studies" (Participant 10; UCLM).

Furthermore, a participant from Warwick pointed out:

"For me it was a great opportunity to get to know more things about the Spanish culture. I enjoy talking every week with someone from a different country" (Participant 24; Warwick).

Similarly, a student from Warwick stated:

"I like to speak Spanish with a native speaker because my weakest points are the listening and the speaking" (Participant 38; Warwick).

The only negative observations were related to the length and timing of connections. Warwick students seemed to have more flexibility in the time available to talk, perhaps due to their familiarity in taking part in virtual exchanges, although one Warwick student commented:

> "The hardest thing was perhaps finding a time to chat! It was difficult finding a time when both of us were available" (Participant 23; Warwick).

3.   Conclusion

In general, both sets of participants enjoyed the tasks and took active part in the project. Moreover, they positively valued the opportunity to meet people from different countries as a way of understanding the kind of cross-cultural realities which emerged during the tasks (food, access to the job market, university life, etc.). Tasks were shown to be appropriate for the learning context and learners' profiles (intermediate foreign language level). It was the first time that most of the participants from UCLM had been involved in a virtual project, but this did not impede their involvement perhaps because they were offered weekly advice by tutors on how to proceed and were also given guidance throughout the tasks. All the previous aspects contributed to the achievement of a successful rate of participation. This will help to shape the format of future virtual exchanges and contribute to both language development and professional skills which are considered important in accessing the world job market.

The main limitation of this study has to do with the relatively small number of participants involved. Nonetheless, as a case study, it has shown the possible language and professional skills benefits related to the former of the virtual exchange experience in this particular setting and with these participants.

References

Chapelle, C. (2001). *Computer applications in second language acquisition.* Cambridge: Cambridge University Press. https://doi.org/10.1017/CBO9781139524681

Council of Europe. (2001). *Common European framework of reference for languages: learning, teaching and assessment.* Cambridge: Cambridge University Press.

Cunningham, D. J., & Vyatkina, N. (2012). Telecollaboration for professional purposes: towards developing a formal register in the foreign language classroom. *Canadian modern language review, 68*(4), 422-450. https://doi.org/10.3138/cmlr.1279

Helm, F., & Guth, S. (2010). The multifarious goals of telecollaboration 2.0: theoretical and practical implications. In S. Guth & F. Helm (Eds) *Telecollaboration 2.0: language, literacy and intercultural learning in the 21st century* (pp. 69-106). Bern: Lang.

Kurek, M. (2015). Designing tasks for complex virtual learning environments. *Bellaterra journal of teaching & learning language & literature, 8*(2), 13-32. https://doi.org/10.5565/rev/jtl3.633

Maynard, D. W. & Peräkylä, A. (2003). Language and social interaction. In S. T. Fiske, D. T. Gilbert & G. Lindzey (Eds) *Handbook of social psychology* (pp. 233-258). New Jersey: John Wiley & Sons.

O'Dowd, R. (2005). Negotiating sociocultural and institutional contexts: the case of Spanish-American telecollaboration. *Language and intercultural communication, 5*(1), 40-56. https://doi.org/10.1080/14708470508668882

O'Dowd, R. (2007). Foreign language and the rise of online communication: a review of promises and realities. In R. O'Dowd (Eds), *Online intercultural exchange: an introduction for foreign language teachers* (pp. 17-40). Clevedon: Multilingual Matters.

O'Dowd, R., & Lewis, T. (Eds). (2016). *Online intercultural exchange: policy, pedagogy, practice.* New York and London: Routledge.

Romaña Correa, Y. (2015). Skype™ Conference Calls: A Way to Promote Speaking Skills in the Teaching and Learning of English. *PROFILE, 17*(1), 143-156. https://doi.org/10.15446/profile.v17n1.41856

7 Content modules in UK and US universities – their unique contribution towards the development of intercultural competence and criticality

Elinor Parks[1]

Abstract

This paper explores the unique contribution of content modules towards the development of criticality (Barnett, 1997) and intercultural competence (Byram, 1997) in Modern Languages (ML). It draws upon the findings of a PhD study investigating the implications of the division between language and content, as experienced by German Studies students in two American and two British universities. Findings from this study echo to an extent Brumfit et al. (2005), who found that in language modules "the focus on criticality development itself is less central than in other areas of the ML curriculum, especially the 'content' courses" (p. 159). In interviews, both staff and students across all four universities referred to upper-level or content modules as the area which contributed the most to students' development of intercultural competence and criticality, yet content-based language courses were also cited. Implications of these findings are discussed and recommendations are made for the future of ML in Higher Education (HE).

Keywords: language degrees, content modules, higher education, criticality, intercultural competence, languages.

1. University of Hull, Hull, United Kingdom; e_parks2@yahoo.com

How to cite this chapter: Parks, E. (2017). Content modules in UK and US universities – their unique contribution towards the development of intercultural competence and criticality . In C. Álvarez-Mayo, A. Gallagher-Brett, & F. Michel (Eds), *Innovative language teaching and learning at university: enhancing employability* (pp. 59-66). Research-publishing.net. https://doi.org/10.14705/rpnet.2017.innoconf2016.655

© 2017 Elinor Parks (CC BY-NC-ND)

1.   Introduction

Culture and literature courses (also referred to as content modules in the UK) are often understood as belonging to the 'area studies' component of ML degrees. These modules provide a context for the critical study of culture and help situate the discipline within the humanities. Yet, as a result of the way language degrees are structured in the UK, as Brumfit et al. (2005) argue, "consideration of the exact nature of the interaction between language and content is often neglected" (p. 158). The teaching of 'language' as a parallel component alongside 'content' has been identified as problematic both in British and American HE. Gieve and Cunico (2012) point out that in the UK it is common to offer grammar and translation classes within language modules, which consist of "texts bearing little or no connection to any of the 'content' modules that run in parallel" (p. 275). While foreign language departments follow a different structure in the US, for the most part consisting of two years of language study (lower-level) followed by two years of content-based language and content classes (upper-level), the separation of language and content has been similarly reported as problematic. The Modern Language Association (MLA, 2007) report makes reference to the issue, arguing that "a two-tiered structure impedes the development of a unified curriculum" and that the foreign language curriculum "should consist of a series of complementary or linked courses that holistically incorporate content and cross-cultural reflection at every level" (p. 5).

The importance of intercultural competence has been further specified in the Quality Assurance Agency (2015) subject Benchmark Statement, suggesting that "students of languages develop awareness of similarities and dissimilarities between other cultures and societies, and their own" (p. 16). This is even more explicitly articulated in the MLA (2007) report, which argues that "the language major should be structured to produce a specific outcome: educated speakers who have deep translingual and transcultural competence" (p. 3), and in the *Review of Modern Foreign Languages provision in higher education in England* (Worton, 2009), arguing that universities should take a more 'active leadership' role by placing emphasis on intercultural competence and multi-lingual skills.

The contribution of content modules towards the development of students' criticality and intercultural competence discussed in this paper has been identified in previous research. Brumfit et al. (2005) reported on a research project (Southampton Project) on criticality development in undergraduate students in two academic disciplines at one British university, one of which was ML. The researchers highlight the important role of content modules in supporting the development of criticality, as mentioned in the abstract, but also point out that it may be "the rich combination of language with cultural content, of learning in the university with acquisition on the year abroad, that may be the valuable contribution being made overall" (Brumfit et al., 2005, p. 161). The value of literature specifically has been acknowledged in Matos (2011), who argues that "literature may help develop an essential feature of the intercultural personality: the ability to decentre and take up the perspectives of the other, to see the world from another place" (p. 2). Phipps and Gonzales (2004) similarly expose the marginalised status of literature within the ML curriculum and argue that it should rather be "central to learning to be intercultural" (p. 138).

Bearing the above theoretical perspectives in mind, this paper provides an overview of staff and student perspectives on the contribution of content modules to the development of intercultural competence (Byram, 1997) and criticality (Barnett, 1997).

2.   Method

2.1.   Participants and setting

The doctoral study, from which the findings are drawn, employed a mixed methods design consisting of a student questionnaire and interviews with students enrolled on the German degree programme and key faculty members. Four institutions agreed to take part in the study, two of which are located in the north of England (Universities A and B) and two in the US (C and D). The universities taking part were given a pseudonym to maintain confidentiality and comply with ethical requirements. The curriculum in place at University A offered all content courses taught in English with language modules (writing and oral components) taught in parallel. At University B, on the other hand, content was taught in German, with the exception of the first year[2]. With regards to the American universities, University C's German department is well-known, as it adopts an innovative genre-based content-oriented curriculum throughout the degree programme. University D, on the other hand, while not having eliminated the two-tiered structure, offers content-based language modules, which similarly appear to offer students a context in which language and content can be taught jointly.

2.2. Data collection, participants and analysis

Questionnaire and interview data was collected over a period of ten weeks in the spring term of 2015. A total of 56 students responded to the questionnaire, and 21 expressed interest in the follow-up interview. A further interview was conducted with seven members of staff across the four universities. Quantitative data was collected through a questionnaire using a six point Likert scale. Interview participants were contacted by mail and the interviews were carried out on the university campuses or through Skype. Interviews were interpreted qualitatively and the questionnaire data was analysed statistically using SPSS. This paper reviews a selection of results, primarily qualitative, which focus on the findings related to the unique contribution of content modules to the development of intercultural competence and criticality among undergraduates/university students.

3. Discussion

While the participating universities differed significantly in their curricula, data drawn from all four institutions indicated that content and upper-level modules played a significant role in the development of students' criticality and intercultural competence. The findings reflect both a student and staff perspective.

2. This was the case at the time of the data collection (in the 2014-2015 academic year).

The Head of German at University B illustrated how these modules played a role in the students' development of these competencies:

> "I think [the development of criticality] is more something that happens in our modules rather than doing it independently. It's rather when you start talking about things… and they are guided through certain texts… that you make them think, then they engage with it".

In the student questionnaire over three-quarters of the participants agreed that content modules provided a greater opportunity to develop a critical awareness of cultures than language modules (Figure 1).

Figure 1. Pie chart: content modules provided a greater opportunity to develop a critical awareness of cultures than language modules.

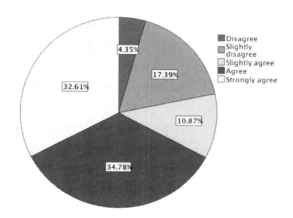

These views were echoed in the follow-up student interviews. Mary, of University B, described topics in the language modules as "superficial" and felt that as a result they could only be critical to a "certain extent":

> "I think it's critical to a certain extent with the language modules […] my problem with the language modules in general is that they tend to be very… I think the German word *oberflächlich* (superficial/shallow)

is quite good. […] If your aim is to teach how to write good German… I don't know… I think with the content modules there was constant challenge of having to go away and research it yourself".

Zak, of University A, also "felt like the teachers were more critical with [him] in the content modules". While content modules were mentioned across all four institutions as contributing to the development of intercultural competence and criticality, reference was also made to the language modules, particularly at University C where the department had redesigned the curriculum in order to address the 'language' and 'content' divide.

JFK, of University C, made reference to how his intermediate German class helped him reflect on the concept of *Heimat* (homeland):

> "From day one, from the first class, I've been learning about the Turkish migration in Germany, differences between East and West, I learned about the concept of *Heimat*. It's already critical".

At University B, the language coordinator, who was teaching both language and content modules as well as coordinating the Year Abroad assessment task, referred to this as an "advantage":

> "I have the advantage of teaching language and content. I've taught 1st year and 2nd year content. Second year content is taught and assessed in German and I found that really interesting because you can really emphasise the links between the topics, the themes that you're talking about in language and content and how they overlap".

The reference above is particularly interesting as it presents a perspective from an academic, who was responsible for teaching both language and content and took this opportunity to establish relevant links across the curriculum. Students' views on whether they felt language and content should be better integrated also differed significantly across the four institutions, as illustrated in Figure 2, ranging from mean values of 5.22 (agree) to 2.78 (between slightly disagree and disagree).

Figure 2.   Mean scores and bar graph – perceived need for greater integration

University A	University D	University B	University C
5.22	4.50	3.35	2.78

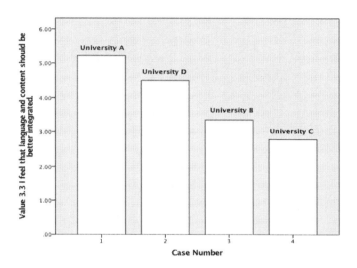

Case Number

4.   Conclusion

The findings suggest that content modules make an invaluable contribution towards student development of criticality and intercultural competence, thus echoing to an extent Brumfit et al. (2005). However, as the results appear to indicate, language modules can also effectively support students' development of these competencies, particularly where faculty have explored ways to establish links across the two curricula and beyond.

The following recommendations are made for ML in HE: firstly, that content modules and upper-level content-based language modules (in the US) be acknowledged as an invaluable context for university-based learning of intercultural skills and criticality; and, secondly, to recognise that the separation of language and content needs to be addressed in order to explore more effective ways of fostering students' criticality and intercultural learning across the entire curriculum.

5.   Acknowledgements

I would like to acknowledge the continuous support received from the University of Hull as well as all the participating institutions that welcomed me and strongly supported my research project.

References

Barnett, R. (1997). *Higher education: a critical business*. Bristol: Open University Press.

Brumfit, C., Myles, F., Mitchell, R., Johnston, B., & Ford, P. (2005). Language study in higher education and the development of criticality. *International journal of applied linguistics, 15*(2), 145-168. https://doi.org/10.1111/j.1473-4192.2005.00085.x

Byram, M. (1997). *Teaching and assessing intercultural communicative competence*. Clevedon: Multilingual Matters.

Gieve, S., & Cunico, S. (2012). Language and content in the modern foreign languages degree: a students' perspective. *The language learning journal, 40*(3), 273-291. https://doi.org/10.1080/09571736.2011.639459

MLA. (2007). *Foreign languages and higher education: new structures for a changed world*. http://www.mla.org/flreport

Matos, A. G. (2011). *Literary texts and intercultural learning: exploring new directions*. Oxford: Peter Lang.

Phipps, A. M., & Gonzales, M. (2004). *Modern languages – learning and teaching in an intercultural field*. London: Sage.

Quality Assurance Agency. (2015). *Subject benchmark statement: languages, cultures and societies*. http://www.qaa.ac.uk/publications/information-and-guidance/publication?PubID=2982#.WHjTdIXgWDo

Worton, M. (2009). *Review of modern foreign languages provisions in higher education in England*. HEFCE. http://webarchive.nationalarchives.gov.uk/20100202100434/http://hefce.ac.uk/pubs/year/2009/200941/

8 Developing intercultural communicative competence for the year abroad experience

Sandra López-Rocha[1] and Fabienne Vailes[2]

Abstract

Intercultural Communication Training (ICT) is crucial in the preparation of students who will study or work abroad as part of their degree programme. The promotion of key competencies will allow students to become aware of different perspectives, develop a more accurate understanding and appreciation of other cultures, and participate more integrally in the host culture.

Keywords: intercultural communicative competence, intercultural training, intercultural citizenship, awareness and attitudes, year abroad preparation.

1.   Introduction

It is a fact that preparation for the Year Abroad facilitates students' adaptation to the host culture (Coleman, 1995) while developing an appreciation for the multi-layered elements of the host environment. This, in turn, translates into a better understanding of the culture, beyond stereotyping and constrained surface observations, a maximisation of their experience, and the development of Intercultural Communicative Competence (ICC). In response to this need, UK higher education institutions are currently promoting ICC skills as part of the pre-departure preparation of students. This paper explores the content and perceived outcomes of a programme aimed at fostering the development

---

1. University of Bristol, Bristol, United Kingdom; s.lopezrocha@bristol.ac.uk

2. University of Bristol, Bristol, United Kingdom; f.vailes@bristol.ac.uk

How to cite this chapter: López-Rocha, S., & Vailes, F. (2017). Developing intercultural communicative competence for the Year Abroad experience. In C. Álvarez-Mayo, A. Gallagher-Brett, & F. Michel (Eds), *Innovative language teaching and learning at university: enhancing employability* (pp. 67-75). Research-publishing.net. https://doi.org/10.14705/rpnet.2017.innoconf2016.656

© 2017 Sandra López-Rocha and Fabienne Vailes (CC BY)

of ICC prior to and during the Year Abroad. In order to achieve this, we will first address the notion of ICC and the development of a training programme implemented at the University of Bristol's School of Modern Languages (SML), providing an overview of the content, an analysis of the students' perceptions of the programme, and suggestions for the future. The overall idea we intend to convey is that a programme of this nature is necessary to foster skills involved in the promotion of intercultural citizenship.

ICC emerged as a specialised field of study of interactions and abilities developed in a foreign country, taking into account the role of foreign languages in the development of skills and attitudes. Byram (2012) has been instrumental in the creation of a framework for the development of ICC integrating *skills* (to interpret, relate, discover, and interact); *knowledge* about the culture and interactions between members of different groups; *attitudes* to enhance self-awareness and appreciation of different cultural tendencies; and, *education* with regards to critical issues in the host culture. Furthermore, the model encompasses intercultural attitudes *(savoir être)* to develop curiosity, openness, and readiness to change views. This model also encourages the development of critical cultural awareness *(savoir s'engager)* in the preparation of knowledgeable individuals able to reflect and engage effectively in a different cultural context. Similarly, Deardorff's (2006) influential model for the development of intercultural competence also promotes self-awareness, openness, and transformation. The pre-departure module currently implemented at the SML strives to align itself within these frameworks in order to enhance the second-year students' preparation for the Year Abroad, additionally incorporating the work of Hall (1997), Hennebry (2014), and Jones (2000).

Besides fostering the development of key intercultural skills, the module also intends to instil awareness with regards to intercultural adaptation and stress. Although it is often seen as a negative element in the process of adjusting to life in a different country, acculturative stress "may indeed have a positive effect on individuals, as it represents a source of constant learning and exposure to intercultural experiences" (López-Rocha, 2014, p. 2270). Furthermore, this process is linked to the development of resilience among students as it involves "adapting well in the face of adversity […] or significant sources of stress, such as family and relationship problems, […] or workplace and financial stressors. It means 'bouncing back' from difficult experiences" (American Psychological Association, 2016, n.p.). The programme is designed to provide students with the opportunity to discover and develop new behaviours, thoughts and actions that they may not have previously considered, enabling them to cope with various situations in the host country, in addition to raising consciousness of the potential effects of reverse-culture shock upon their return to the UK.

2.   Programme content

The pilot programme, involving over 240 students of French and Spanish, consisted of a 4-week module implemented in the second part of their second year at university, prior to starting the third Year Abroad. Each week, the students participated in a one-hour seminar requiring some preparatory work (e.g. reading scenarios, answering questions and completing worksheets), as well as some follow-up tasks (e.g. reflecting on what was discussed and participating in a virtual site).

The sessions encompassed the introduction of ICC theory and practical exercises, directly drawing from and building on the students' own experience. Classroom dynamics provided the opportunity for tutor-student open interactions, as well as for pair/group discussions and role-play.

In the first session, the notions of culture and ICC were explored, introducing the idea of culture-specific attributes and the value of considering different perspectives.

The second session focused on potential sources of intercultural conflict, adaptation, and culture shock, involving critical narratives based on experiences reported by our own students while abroad, to identify ways of addressing issues from different perspectives.

In the third session, we discussed the deconstruction of stereotypes and promoted the idea of cultural tendencies as a more accurate way to describe cultures, behaviours, and attitudes; furthermore, students explored differences in non-verbal communication, allowing for a discussion on preconceptions, perceptions of the self by others, and our natural tendency to interpret different behaviours based on our own values and beliefs. In the final session the students explored the way in which different attitudes influence interactions, received country-specific information, and further recommendations. Figure 1, Figure 2, Figure 3, and Figure 4 below provide an overview of some of the materials used.

Figure 1.   Week 1 – Students' group postings on *Padlet*

WHAT IS CULTURE?
1. Individually - write what you understand by culture. 2. Share it with the rest of your group. 3. Input a maximum of 3 items on this page.

Way of thinking, different perspective of life, how a community goes about daily life

social conventions

Food

Traditions, the way people act, what separates groups of people

etiquete
etiquete is key
food, music, dancing

The way a country expresses itself

the arts and other manifestations of human intellectual achievement regarded collectively.
"20th century popular culture"
synonyms: the arts, the humanities;
More
2.
the ideas, customs, and social behaviour of a particular people or society.
"Afro-Caribbean culture"
synonyms: civilization, society, way of life, lifestyle; More

CMB
What's unique to a country or a group of people

Different norms of societies n ting:)

Missy duck
What people look like and what their memes are

Emily and Zoe
The language and lifestyle of the local people e.g. food, daily routine, music etc

Culture
Values, ways of communicating, dealing with things

·A
Music

Books music history art

Alex
The individual style of a community

food, language, religion, customs, identity

Kim K
FOOOOD
Language
Traditions

History, language and traditions/customs.
Bob

background, climate, language, food, culture, traditions.... and the way people react to it

Customs

CeCe
Tradition, Social norms, Lifestyle

Highlandspring
perspective of life/lifestyle

Language, traditions customs

Cool group
Traditions, behaviour, language, values

Different customs

Mills and Holly
Language, Histroy, Art,

Culture is the traditions and norms in another country

Culture
Traditions, politics & behaviour

Art, music, dance, religion, history!

HAM
Traditions, behaviour food.

Mario, Cesar, Mimi
Culture is everything that surrounds us

Figure 2.   Week 2 – Advice and support for dealing with culture shock

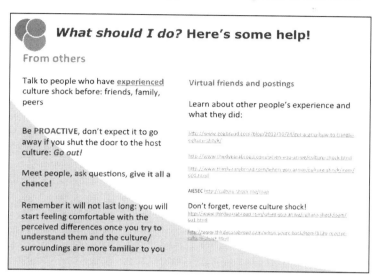

Figure 3.   Week 3 – Follow-up discussion after a role-play activity on non-verbal communication

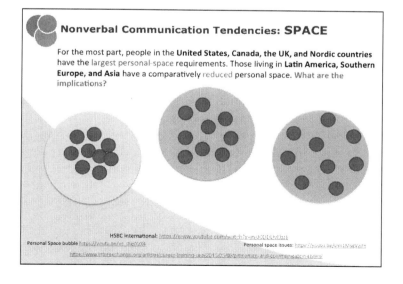

Figure 4. Week 4 – Overview of topics covered in the module

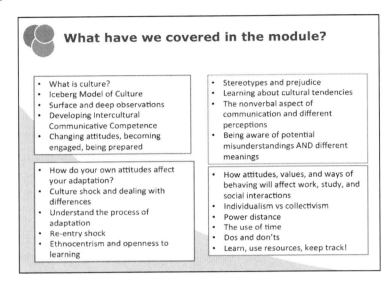

3. Outcomes

On completion of the module, the students were invited to participate anonymously in an online survey consisting of 14 items combining Likert scales and open-ended questions focused on evaluating the module's content, form of delivery and relevance for the Year Abroad. The overall results were indeed positive, although the fact that feedback was non-mandatory influenced the survey return rate as only 9% of the attendees responded. Nevertheless, the data still provided a good insight into how the programme was received. The quantified answers indicate that 68% of respondents attended three or four sessions, an encouraging number considering that these were an addition to their scheduled classes and took place towards the end of the teaching block, when students are engaged in revision for their final assessments. 73% of the respondents found being allowed to share their views in the sessions engaging. In addition, a combined 68% of students described the sessions useful, very useful, and extremely useful. Moreover, 60% of participants indicated that this training should be a mandatory part of the preparation for the Year Abroad, while 77% stated that they would certainly recommend others to take the module. There is also an indication of consistency with the programme's objectives, as students identified skills they started to develop as a direct result of taking the module, namely an increase in intercultural awareness, a feeling of an improved adaptability in combination with a potential minimisation of culture shock, the development of skills involving intercultural competence, a better management of expectations, and a greater confidence to deal with intercultural issues. Furthermore, students were able to address specific aspects of ICC, such as the complexity behind the notion of culture and the importance of developing intercultural competence. Students also highlighted other factors as particularly positive, including content, the interactivity of the classroom dynamics and tasks, sustained interest, reassurance, and the tutors' friendliness and approachability.

Developing and implementing a programme of this nature has a number of challenges. Some of these involve helping students to more accurately understand and appreciate the development of ICC, not only for the Year Abroad, but also as part of the development of intercultural citizenship. This is also linked to the fact that ICC cannot be completely acquired; students will develop their own skills, learn about the host culture, and change their attitudes at their own pace. Although this programme is intended to provide the basis for the development of specific skills (c.f. Byram, 2012), ideally, it should be more integrally contextualised in terms of specific countries and sub-regions. This would require year-long units dedicated to particular aspects of intercultural communication, for instance, within a given sociolinguistic, communicative or ethnographic perspective, which requires the module leader to have a strong background in intercultural communication and related fields. Finally, students at this stage of preparation for the Year Abroad seem to be more concerned with immediate needs involving logistic matters, from securing a visa to finding accommodation. This became evident whilst analysing the results, as students were interested in what they considered 'urgent' matters and expected tutors to provide them with country-specific information involving those specific *how-to* items.

4.   Future directions

Based on the results, the module will continue to be implemented with some adjustments. For instance, prior to the start, information on logistic matters will be made available giving students access to a live database where previous Year Abroad undergraduates have input relevant information and shared their experiences. This has already proved useful for those currently preparing for their Year Abroad, allowing them to first address what they consider their 'immediate needs', and to later focus on the ICC module's content and tasks. The intended objectives will be provided prior to the start of the module to ensure that students have realistic expectations of content and intended outcomes.

In addition, returning Year Abroad students will also be invited to take part in some of the sessions (they currently attend general Year Abroad information sessions to share their experience working or studying abroad), giving second-year students an opportunity to more directly relate to their peers' experiences.

Finally, to provide further information beyond Spanish and French students, a collection of critical incidents, involving languages taught at a degree level at the University of Bristol's SML, will be created to explore values at work, in university settings and in social contexts, as well as situations requiring adaptation and problem-solving strategies, among others.

Our aim for the long term is to continue expanding the module to include all languages offered at the SML. Ideally, this will develop into a year-long formal unit for second-year students that would truly enable participants to embed the skills and knowledge presented in the module. Furthermore, we strongly believe there is an urgent need for ICC training to be included in the curriculum at the start of undergraduate studies and continued on to final-year studies, where critical topics in intercultural communication could be studied at an advanced level, integrating the students' acquired knowledge and perspectives from the Year Abroad.

References

American Psychological Association. (2016). *The road to resilience.* http://www.apa.org/helpcenter/road-resilience.aspx

Byram, M. (2012). Conceptualizing intercultural (communicative) competence and intercultural citizenship. In J. Jackson (Ed.) *The Routledge handbook of language and intercultural communication* (pp. 85-97). London: Routledge.

Coleman, J. (1995). The current state of knowledge concerning student residence abroad. In G. Parker & A. Rouxeville (Eds), *The Year Abroad: preparation, monitoring, evaluation.* London: AFLS/CILT.

Deardorff, D. K. (2006). Identification and assessment of intercultural competence as a student outcome of internationalization. *Journal of studies in international education, 10*(3), 241-266. http://dx.doi.org/10.1177/1028315306287002

Hall, E. T. (1997). *Beyond culture.* New York: Anchor Books.

Hennebry, M. (2014). Cultural awareness: should it be taught? Can it be taught? In P. Driscoll, E. Macaro & A. Swarbrick (Eds), *Debates in modern languages education* (pp. 135-150). London: Routledge.

Jones, B. (2000). Developing cultural awareness. In K. Field (Ed.), *Issues in modern foreign languages teaching* (pp. 151-162). London: Routledge.

López-Rocha, S. (2014). Stress and acculturation. In W. Cockerham, R. Dingwall & S. Quah (Eds), *The Wiley Blackwell encyclopedia of health, illness, behavior, and society* (pp. 2270-2272). Chicester: John Wiley & Sons. https://doi.org/10.1002/9781118410868.wbehibs123

Section 3.

Fostering employability
in the classroom

9 Rotating poster presentations

Manuel Lagares[1] and Sandra Reisenleutner[2]

Abstract

Oral presentations are a common practice in foreign language classes, often used to assess students' speaking skills. Usually, the presentations are delivered by students in front of the class, often with PowerPoint slides or Prezi as support. However, frequently the audience does not engage with the presentation and thus, the benefits of this format are somewhat limited and imbalanced. In addition, the prospect for the student of spending several weeks just sitting and listening to others' presentations does not have a motivational effect. For these reasons, Rotating Poster Presentations (RPP), refurbished formats of oral presentations, were introduced in German and Spanish language classes at the University of Nottingham. Students created a poster as support for their presentation. The setup of the presentation was based on the idea of a fair, where students interact with the various presenters. This model led to very positive student feedback. Participants found it easier to present their topics, as small group interaction contributed to increased confidence. Besides, the audience was much more motivated to attend the classes and the interaction between presenters and audience gained in quality. Students found the poster presentations clearer and engaging. Moreover, the format of the fair, the creation of the poster, the need for exact time-management, the focus of autonomous and student-led work, as well as the tasks and the presentation, are transferable skills that go beyond the language classroom.

1. University of Nottingham, Nottingham, United Kingdom; Manuel.Lagares@nottingham.ac.uk

2. University of Nottingham, Nottingham, United Kingdom; Sandra.Reisenleutner@nottingham.ac.uk

How to cite this chapter: Lagares, M., & Reisenleutner, S. (2017). Rotating poster presentations. In C. Álvarez-Mayo, A. Gallagher-Brett, & F. Michel (Eds), *Innovative language teaching and learning at university: enhancing employability* (pp. 79-87). Research-publishing.net. https://doi.org/10.14705/rpnet.2017.innoconf2016.657

© 2017 Manuel Lagares and Sandra Reisenleutner (CC BY)

Keywords: poster presentations, oral presentations, interaction, motivation, creativity, autonomous learning, evaluation of speaking skills, employability.

1.   Introduction

Oral presentations are a common practice in language classes. The learning objectives are to focus on speaking and presentation skills and to support research in a certain area. Students need to prove that they can speak in a foreign language in front of an audience and that they are able to transmit ideas clearly. Ideally, they apply already learnt language skills and develop them further through independent study during the preparation process. Presentations are also a common format for assessing oral skills, and for this reason class time is generously used to hold students' presentations.

Setting the learning objectives for the audience seems, on the other hand, less straightforward. The attending students are expected to listen to the presentations and might pose a question to the speaker. Teachers would like them to learn something new about the topics, other presentation methods and even new words or structures. However, this is very hard to monitor without an assessment, a quiz or a thorough discussion engaging all the participants after the presentations – something that might not be possible due to time constraints. Besides, teachers would like their students to enjoy the presentations and have a more active role.

In reality, many teachers will also have observed that the audience does not always pay attention to the presentation and does not engage in a discussion afterwards. Furthermore, attendance rates during presentation weeks tend to drop as students lack motivation to come to class. When the whole presentation is summative, the listeners and fellow classmates are even more reluctant to ask a question by fear of placing the presenter into a difficult situation. Thus, one of the aims of this project was to foster more interaction during presentations.

2.   Rotating poster presentations

In academic conferences, poster presentations are a common way of sharing research. In oral presentations delivered by students in language classes, the visual support usually comes from software like PowerPoint or Prezi. However, these have disadvantages that are relevant to this project: particularly, the fact that only one presentation can take place at a time. After revising the concept of poster presentations to make it relevant for the foreign language classroom, this new model, called RPP, was introduced in four modules at the University of Nottingham: two German language modules at A2 level and two Spanish language modules at B1 level. In the German module, students delivered a presentation as part of their formative assessment. In the Spanish modules, the presentations counted towards the final grade.

The activity given to students incorporated many elements that Dörnyei (2014) names as crucial to increase learner motivation. In his discussion of motivational practices focusing on the individual learner level, Dörnyei (2014, p. 526) names "breaking the monotony of learning" and "making the learning task more interesting" as some of the key features to enhance motivation. The RPP posed a challenge, offered a tangible outcome, added a novelty element and linked personal interest with content. Other motivational practices such as "increasing the learner's self-confidence" can be applied to this model as students present the posters several times in front of small groups, which decreases the face-threatening environment.

Furthermore, the format and tasks posed fostered the development of various transferable skills.

2.1.   The format of the RPP

Students were given a series of topics and had to create a five-minute oral presentation about one of them. In addition to the presentation, they were required to create a poster to visually support their presentation.

The presentation itself followed a specific routine that is similar to that of a fair, where students walk around, listen to the various presentations being delivered at the same time and interact with the presenters. A typical setup for a Spanish B1 class with twelve students would be as follows:

- The tutor distributes the topics and the dates two to three weeks in advance. All presentations take place within four weeks, three students presenting each week.

- On presentation day, the tutor divides the audience into three groups.

- The three presenters hang their posters in different parts of the room as all of them address a different audience at the same time.

- The audience rotates around the room from presenter to presenter in order to listen to all the presentations.

- After each presentation, the listeners ask questions to the speakers for an additional five minutes.

- Then, they move on to the next speaker and a new cycle of presentations starts.

- The teacher rotates in the opposite direction, in order to join a different group of listeners.

Figure 1 shows a graphic explanation of this method.

Another possible setup would be to deliver all presentations in just one session of one hour. This was successfully used in the German A2 project, where students voted for their favourite poster at the end. This element of friendly "intragroup competition", also discussed by Dörnyei (2001, pp. 43-45), works towards building a cohesive group and promotes "intermember relationships", which in return increase motivation in language learning.

Figure 1. The specific routine

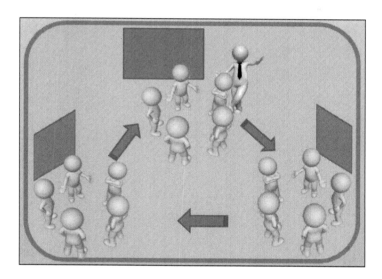

2.2. The choice of topics

The topics in both modules were selected so that students would find them engaging and motivating: therefore, the focus was placed on creative and non-controversial topics. We judged that talking about contentious issues could impact negatively on the presenter's performance and the audience's attention as much as the other external affective factors that Martínez Baztán (2011) describes in his discussion of 'communicative stress': the factors that influence negatively a speech producing ambiguity or linguistic or pragmatic mistakes.

The students were expected to work in an innovative way, develop their ideas further and formulate them in their own words. They were required to defend their choices and persuade the audience – both important functions at A2 and B1 levels, according to the Common European Framework of Reference for languages (CEFR).

Figure 2 shows sample topics for both levels.

Figure 2.   Sample topics for the B1 (left) and the A2 (right) modules

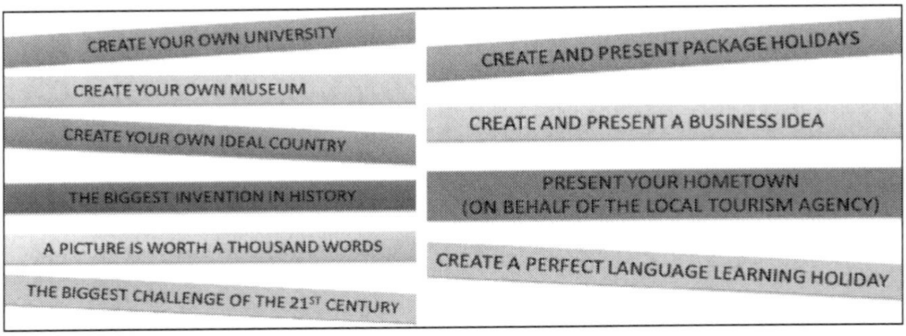

2.3.   The nature of the tasks

In the German A2 modules, the topics were aligned with the class content as the students' language repertoire was limited; in the Spanish B1 modules the topics were broader. From a methodical perspective, the RPP are largely based on a task-based approach. According to Nunan (2004), a task "involves learners in comprehending, manipulating, producing or interacting in the target language" (p. 4). A crucial element in his definition is that students' language knowledge is activated to express meaning. In both modules, students had to create a product and successfully present it to their audience, characteristics mentioned by Willis and Willis (2007) in their definition of tasks.

The way of presenting the products followed the same patterns in both projects. However, while in the A2 RPP, the students were given a task and had to prepare their posters in groups of two to three, in the B1 RPP, they worked individually due to the requirements of the assessment.

2.4.   Different ways of adapting
this model and assessment

The RPP model can be used as formative and summative assessment. The latter was chosen for the B1 Spanish modules, while in the A2 German modules students received formative feedback.

In assessed RPP, the order in which the tutor listens to the speakers must be discussed with the students beforehand. Alternatively, students can use the first round for practice instead of starting immediately with assessed presentations.

From the assessment perspective, the question and answer phase after the formal presentation is at least as interesting as the former. As the speaker and the audience interact in a more spontaneous way, the speaker will switch between planned and unplanned discourse, letting the tutor evaluate more accurately the real stage of the student's learning process (Ellis, 2004).

For non-assessed RPP, the group work proved popular with students. As Dooly (2008) recommends in the context of student's interaction, it fostered a sense of common achievement as the outcome could only be successful if everyone contributed to the task.

Depending on the module requirements or aims, students may be asked to work on different or identical topics. The former undoubtedly increases the interest of the audience, especially for topic-based presentations. However, we have also observed positive results on the latter when working with marketing and advertisement presentations, as this makes it easier to compare different degrees of performance.

3.   Conclusion

The benefits of introducing RPP in the foreign language classroom have been numerous.

The RPP model enhances motivation to come to class and speak. Students maintain interest and the whole class participates actively, providing students with the opportunity to practise asking questions. The movement around the classroom helps students maintain concentration. Working in small groups requires them to pay more attention and become attentive and active listeners – two concepts that are not always practised during presentations. For the presenters, who often give their first presentation in the foreign language, these small groups reduce the affective filter as the context becomes less intimidating (Laine, 1988). The format of the RPP makes it easier to follow the presentations, while posters act as prompts for the presenters. Moreover, there is a fundamental change compared to the usual presentation in class: the presentations are repeated to different audiences, thus boosting the confidence and motivation of the students by practising it a number of times, and if necessary, students can make minor adjustments to each presentation. Besides, repetition can contribute to some improvement in fluency and accuracy, as described by Bygate (1996).

Another crucial aspect of the RPP model is the focus on autonomous learning: students have to work independently as the tutor can only stay with one group at a time. Hence, responsibility is shared and the class needs to work together to achieve a successful outcome. Exact time management is crucial, as groups need to swap after delivering their presentation and answering questions.

Overall, the advantages observed, as well as the very positive student feedback, have led us to introduce the model to more modules and develop it further. After evaluating the pilot project, we would like to add two aspects in the future: a session on how to formulate questions correctly, before the presentations are held; and a follow-up session to analyse common mistakes and very relevant questions.

The model has worked very well in the context of language teaching and there is still scope for further development, as the presentations will differ with any group or setting. The task-based approach, the room for creativity and student interaction, the need for cooperation and the final product led to higher learner motivation.

Finally, the development of skills like team-work, collaborative problem solving and decision making, communication in a foreign language, time-management, creating a research poster, or talking in front of an audience enhances the employability profile of the participating students.

References

Bygate, M. (1996). Effects of task repetition: appraising the developing language of learners. In J. Willis & D. Willis (Eds), *Challenge and change in language teaching* (pp. 136-146). Oxford: Heinemann.

Dooly, M. (2008). Understanding the many steps for effective collaborative language projects. *The Language Learning Journal, 36*(1), 65-78. https://doi.org/10.1080/09571730801988405

Dörnyei, Z. (2001). *Motivational strategies in the language classroom.* Cambridge: Cambridge University Press. https://doi.org/10.1017/CBO9780511667343

Dörnyei, Z. (2014). Motivation in second language learning. In M. Celce-Murcia, D. M. Brinton & M. A. Snow (Eds), *Teaching English as a second or foreign language 4th ed.,* (pp. 518-531). Boston, MA: National Geographic Learning/Cengage Learning.

Ellis, R. (2004). The definition and measurement of L2 explicit knowledge. *The Language Learning Journal, 54*(2), 227-275. https://doi.org/10.1111/j.1467-9922.2004.00255.x

Laine, E. (1988). *The affective filter in foreign language learning and teaching.* http://files. eric.ed.gov/fulltext/ED303992.pdf

Martínez Baztán, A. (2011). *La evaluación de las lenguas* (pp. 148-149). Granada: Editorial Octaedro Andalucía.

Nunan, D. (2004). *Task-based language teaching.* Cambridge: Cambridge University Press. https://doi.org/10.1017/CBO9780511667336

Willis, J., & Willis, D. (2007). *Doing task-based teaching.* Oxford: Oxford University Press.

10 Enhancing students' potential: EBL projects in language teaching

Theresa Federici[1]

Abstract

This paper outlines the rationale behind L2 process writing and Enquiry-Based Learning (EBL) approaches adopted in order to design a course within a modern language degree to bridge the gap between language and culture elements of the programme. This was achieved by creating an environment that replicates that of a researcher and by placing feedback and student enquiry at the centre of the language classroom. The approach adopted allows students to engage with techniques of critical thinking and analysis that foster deep-level learning and encourage transferable skills that develop professional skills and increase employability.

Keywords: Enquiry-Based Learning, EBL, process writing, L2 writing, L2 pedagogy.

1.   Introduction

Individual learner identity and the creation of an L2-self are fundamental to successful language acquisition in modern foreign languages degree programmes, enhancing intrinsic and extrinsic motivation towards the language. However, opportunities for genuine self-expression on a topic of personal interest in L2 teaching are rare.

1. Cardiff University, Cardiff, United Kingdom; FedericiT@cardiff.ac.uk

How to cite this chapter: Federici, T. (2017). Enhancing students' potential: EBL projects in language teaching. In C. Álvarez-Mayo, A. Gallagher-Brett, & F. Michel (Eds), *Innovative language teaching and learning at university: enhancing employability* (pp. 89-95). Research-publishing.net. https://doi.org/10.14705/rpnet.2017.innoconf2016.658

© 2017 Theresa Federici (CC BY)

All too often, students reach university with a grade-centred attitude to learning that gives a central role to that all important percentage mark at the end of the course. This attitude inhibits the role of experiential learning, enquiry, self-assessment and reflection on the part of the learner.

Feedback at a formative stage that enables the students to re-engage with their work before the final submission is fundamental in shifting this grade-oriented attitude. To achieve a balance between formative and summative feedback, I created a learning environment that encourages students to reflect on their learning and engage with what they have achieved in order to improve. Through reflecting on research in language pedagogy and my own teaching practice, I adopted a process-driven EBL approach with an emphasis on feedback.

This paper discusses the pedagogical foundations I adopted to implement a communicative language course centred on the writing of individual extended L2 essays and outlines some of the outcomes.

2.   Process writing in language teaching

In many language courses, writing is frequently relegated to a homework activity and is used as a form of consolidation of learning grammatical structures or vocabulary. Though this focus on sentence-level correction is useful in terms of allowing the teacher to diagnose problem areas, relegating writing skills to this position raises several issues. Firstly, the written product focuses on sentence-level accuracy rather than composition and communication. Secondly, students are not presented with a communicative purpose for writing. A process approach aims to address these issues. By bringing the process of composition into the classroom through discussion and collaborative learning, and by setting activities with a genuine readership in mind, writing becomes an integral part of a communicative language-learning environment (Hedge, 1988; Klapper, 2006). By teaching writing as a skill in itself, students are able to develop transferable skills and learning strategies that they can apply to other academic disciplines and to professional situations. Hedge (1988) emphasized the importance of effective, reader-based writing as a core language skill – it requires "a high degree of organization in the development of ideas and information; a high degree of accuracy so that there is no ambiguity of meaning; the use of complex grammatical devices for focus and emphasis; and a careful choice of vocabulary, grammatical patterns, and sentence structures to create a style which is appropriate to the subject matter and the eventual readers" (Hedge, 1988, p. 5).

The process writing approach also encourages students to develop independent learning strategies, as its underlying principle is that students "work out their own solutions to the problems they set themselves" (White & Arndt, 1991, p. 5). White and Arndt (1991) detail the interrelated stages of the approach, such as generating ideas, evaluating, drafting, structuring, focusing, and reviewing. Students work collaboratively through each stage with an emphasis on reflecting on their own work and re-editing and redrafting before reaching the final version.

Process-writing projects can be introduced to language classrooms by presenting students with realistic scenarios or tasks; the facilitator then assists the collaborative generation of ideas and provides guidance as necessary throughout the process with feedback at various draft stages. The students are central to the learning process, whether the outcomes are assessed individually or as a group.

The benefits of a process approach to writing are not just based in language skills. Students further develop collaborative and teamwork skills by working together to generate ideas; these skills are transferable to other disciplines and to professional environments. Students develop the skills in a realistic context with a sense of writing for a purpose and for a specific readership which in turn encourages them to develop a sense of responsibility towards their final draft.

3.   Enquiry-based learning

The methodological approaches informing EBL are very similar to, and indeed overlap significantly with, problem-based learning approaches. Both approaches have their origins in professional training and are frequently employed in scientific disciplines. The semantic difference with EBL is the focus on enquiry rather than problem solving. EBL does not assume that there is one best way to approach a scenario – in fact, a good way to describe an EBL approach to teaching is that it mimics approaches undertaken in research. As with process writing, the emphasis is placed on collaborative learning and the generation of ideas, focusing on heuristic techniques to stimulate research and debate. Both approaches also focus on self-assessment and evaluation with different sources of feedback throughout the sequence. The key element of communality within the approaches is that the process by which the end product is created is as important as the end product itself.

4.   Feedback and assessment

In combining the similar approaches offered by process writing and EBL, I felt it was crucial to create continuity with the forms of assessment. I therefore devised a formative feedback system that would allow students to receive feedback from peers and from the facilitator at regular intervals throughout the project and think critically and reflectively on their work using a self-assessment sheet. Students were asked to self- and peer-assess regularly as an intrinsic element of the class time. Students were formatively assessed on their written production – abstracts, overviews, posters and reviews – and oral production – poster presentations, conference papers and debates. The self-assessment elements enabled students to think about their language accuracy and also their clarity, structure, coherence, and delivery. The peer-assessment encouraged students to develop a genuine sense of readership/audience as they were out of the comfort zone of writing exclusively and privately for the marker. As a result, students tended to put greater emphasis on reader/audience knowledge because they were writing for a genuine purpose, creating reader-appropriate texts, and took greater care in terms of accuracy, syntax, and coherence. Students developed their skills as critical and independent thinkers in their analyses of each other's work and team-building skills when providing constructive and meaningful feedback to peers. The formative facilitator assessment, focused on constructive guidance with an indication of performance but no percentage mark, again simulated the professional environment.

5.   Language acquisition and language pedagogy

A project-based course provides the students with a realistic scenario for writing and gives the students a genuine sense of readership. The importance of setting tasks which are, or are similar to, authentic uses of writing for communication is a crucially important factor in this approach. Students feel that they are writing for a reason and not just to prove to their teacher that they have understood a particular part of the course or a particular grammar point. When going through the planning stages, students are encouraged to consider their readership, the culture, age, interest and knowledge the readership may have of the issues and therefore to consider the appropriate style, register, lexical range and complexity of the written work. The use of the combination of approaches I have adopted creates a non-linear strategy in which each student/author is responsible for reflecting on her/his own work and redrafting and reorganising as s/he thinks appropriate. This idea of returning to one's own work is essential as it helps instil in the students a sense of pride in their work. Word and sentence level language skills are not minimised but are crucial to successful written communication, and, at the same time, these skills are contextualised within a realistic scenario, thus preparing students for writing in the Target Language (TL) outside the academic environment. This approach assists students in establishing an L2 identity and style that is distinct from their L1 identity. It can also address issues of writer-anxiety by giving students the opportunity to experiment with text creation in the TL. As students experiment with and begin to create their L2 literary identity from within the safety of a system that provides feedback and guidance at formative stages, the barriers of apprehension and anxiety that may be present in a composition-based task, regardless of language, break down. Students therefore gain confidence and mastery of self-expression, analysis and research within the L2 writing process, and by experimenting with a variety of literary voices, the students arrive at an outcome that greatly exceeds the aims of the project; the creation of their L2 self. Furthermore, this approach, which mirrors the process of research, with a focus on self-reflection, feedback, dissemination, and redrafting, enables students to locate the skills they gain on this extended writing project within a wider context of transferable, professional, and research skills. Through TL independent writing, critical analysis, and reflection, skills that are both desirable and relevant to communicating in the workplace, students are better equipped to interact using their language skills in professional environments by increasing self-assurance in both spoken and written communication.

6.   Outcomes

The case study of this approach with Year 2 Advanced language learners (ten students), was implemented with a two hour fortnightly session over the 22 teaching weeks. The summative outcome was the submission of a 2,000-word independent research project in L2 and an oral examination in the form of a conference presentation of the research. Students agreed to be interviewed to provide qualitative data for the case study.

By analysing student responses together with their performance over the course of the module, I identified key factors in the success of this model. These factors were: student involvement in the learning process; language skill development; collaborative learning; transferable and professional skills' development perceived by the students; sense of personal achievement; and shifts in self-image and self-belief. I wanted to bring together the notion of 'threshold concepts' (Meyer & Land, 2003), with the shifts in self-perception and learner-identity described in Dornyei (2005). Threshold concepts lead to an irreversible shift in thinking. These concepts are transformative; students' perception of their subject is changed. A similar transformative shift is perceptible when students move from considering themselves as learners, to a concept of themselves as language practitioners able to interact proficiently with L1 speakers. The methodological approaches I adopted to create this experimental project were intended to challenge students' perceptions of language learning and avoid surface learning approaches (Ramsden, 2003).

The freedom of choice and methodology within the project allowed students to challenge themselves in different ways. The 'threshold concepts' elicited by the project have been individual rather than discipline-specific thresholds. The student-driven content of the project gave students the opportunity to challenge their prior knowledge and previous ideas about their own capacities and abilities. This transformative effect, though different in each student, empowered the students to grow and change their sense of identity and self-belief not just within the confines of language learning but on a wider, cognitive scale. It gave them the space to develop from L2 learners to L2 users and thinkers, confident to express themselves in a wide range of verbal and written contexts, and thus enhanced their preparedness for professional environments.

References

Dornyei, Z. (2005). *The psychology of the language learner*. London and New York: Routledge.

Hedge, T. (1988). *Writing*. Oxford: Oxford University Press.

Klapper, J. (2006). *Understanding and developing good practice: teaching languages in higher education*. London: CiLT.

Meyer, J., & Land, R. (2003). Threshold concepts and troublesome knowledge: linkages to ways of thinking and practicing within the disciplines. *ELT Project, Occasional Report 4*.

Ramsden, P. (2003). *Learning to teach in higher education*. New York: RoutledgeFalmer.

White, R., & V. Arndt. (1991). *Process writing*. London: Longman.

11 Using assessment to showcase employability in IWLP

Caroline Campbell[1]

Abstract

Assessment is a critical part of teaching and learning so it is important that students are encouraged to engage positively with it. The Institution-Wide Language Programme (IWLP) at the University of Leeds redesigned its model of assessment for modules at upper-intermediate and advanced levels, broadly equivalent to the Common European Framework of Reference for languages (CEFR) B2-C1, to enable students to develop and evidence their academic skills – such as research skills, digital skills and critical thinking – and to showcase employability behaviours in addition to their language skills and intercultural awareness. This paper outlines the drivers for reviewing the assessment model, explains the design of the new speaking assessment and how this enhances their learning and employability, and provides a brief evaluation of the pilot.

Keywords: assessment, employability, evidence, academic skills, digital skills.

1. Context

This paper explains the rationale for revisiting the IWLP model of assessment, explains the outcomes and provides a brief evaluation. In reviewing the assessment of the credit-bearing modules at CEFR B2-C1, there were four key drivers:

1. University of Leeds, Leeds, United Kingdom; c.campbell@leeds.ac.uk

How to cite this chapter: Campbell, C. (2017). Using assessment to showcase employability in IWLP. In C. Álvarez-Mayo, A. Gallagher-Brett, & F. Michel (Eds), *Innovative language teaching and learning at university: enhancing employability* (pp. 97-104). Research-publishing.net. https://doi.org/10.14705/rpnet.2017.innoconf2016.659

© 2017 Caroline Campbell (CC BY)

- to respond to the University's principle of 'less assessment done better';

- to successfully engage students with the assessment;

- to integrate the development of academic skills;

- to provide evidence of these skills to prospective employers.

In responding to the principle of 'less assessment done better', the model of assessment was reduced from five components to three (see Table 1). Students are often strategic when it comes to assessment – they take into account the weighting of each assessment, to the point of deciding whether or not to sit individual components. This seems to confirm Boud and Falchikov's (2007) observation that

> "[a]ssessment, rather than teaching, has a major influence on students' learning. It directs attention to what is important. It acts as an incentive for study. And it has a powerful effect on what students do and how they do it" (p. 4).

Streamlining the model of assessment (Table 1) resulted in each of the three components having a weighting of at least 30%. It was hoped that this would encourage students to engage positively with each component given the significance of the weighting.

The IWLP modules are offered as 'discovery' modules as part of *broadening*, a key part of the Leeds Curriculum, and they fall within the 'Language and Intercultural Understanding' and 'Personal and Professional Development' *discovery themes*. Students can broaden their skills and intellectual horizons by choosing modules from different disciplines as part of their degree. We reviewed the skills developed on the modules in this context and identified opportunities to develop some of the University's graduate attributes[2]. The

---

2. https://leedsforlife.leeds.ac.uk/skills.aspx

new assessment (1) integrates the development of these skills to complement the learning outcomes, which focus on linguistic development and cultural awareness, and (2) seeks to encourage 'productive learning activity' (Gibbs & Simpson, 2004-05) by highlighting the relevance of students being able to use the language. We also wanted students to have evidence of their skills which they could show to an employer, and this presented an opportunity for students to develop their digital skills. These were the key criteria in designing the speaking task.

Table 1. Models of assessment

Previous model		
Portfolio – individual	Semester 1	25%
Project – individual Reading task 10% Presentation 15% Writing task 20%	Semester 2	45%
Speaking exam – individual	Exam period	30%

New model		
Speaking task – group	Semester 1	35%
Writing task – individual	Semester 2	35%
Speaking exam – individual	Exam period	30%

2.   Designing the speaking task

The term 'speaking task' is used to indicate that students are not expected to give a standard presentation. The task requires them to:

- work in groups;

- research a topic linked to their discipline and/or an aspect of cultural interest linked to the target language;

- demonstrate critical thinking in their analysis;

- present their findings using their choice of media – preferably digital media although this was not a requirement. This encourages them to become familiar with the digital tools available and offers the added benefit of pre-recording the presentation instead of presenting live in the lesson.

Students have the freedom to be creative within the task guidelines. There is flexibility with the choice of topic and the media they use to present their work. The task requires interactivity and this is reflected in the marking criteria: a group mark is given for 'task completion & delivery' and 'content & organisation' and an individual mark for 'use of language' and 'pronunciation & intonation' (Table 2).

Table 2.   Speaking task marking criteria

Group mark	Individual mark
Task completion & delivery	Use of language
Content & organisation	Pronunciation, intonation & fluency

In addition to their linguistic ability, the task outcome enables students to demonstrate a range of skills such as research skills, critical thinking, teamwork, digital skills, and intercultural awareness, all of which employers are keen to see. Using digital media allows them to showcase these skills by uploading a link to their digital profile. Hitherto assessments have been recorded in class but have not been made available to the students. The new task gives students ownership and adds an extra dimension to the assessment.

When designing the speaking task, it was important to consider the influence of assessment on student learning and in particular the effect of 'backwash':

> "Students learn what they think they will be tested on. This is *backwash,* a term coined by Lewis Elton (1987, p. 92), to refer to the effects assessment has on student learning. Assessment determines what and how students learn more than the curriculum does" (Biggs & Tang, 2011, p. 197).

With this in mind, there was an opportunity to develop a student-led assessment which would give students greater freedom and encourage active learning. This represented a deliberate move from tutor-led to student-led assessment. It would give students greater responsibility for their learning and, it was hoped, foster a high level of engagement with the teaching and learning from the start of the module given the nature of the assessment task, the weighting of 35% and its timing to the end of Semester 1. This reflects a conscious effort to empower students by handing over responsibility for their response to the assessment with simply the task outline and marking criteria for guidance. Students are however required to submit a draft proposal – this provides an opportunity for discussion with their tutor and acts as a check regarding, for example, the suitability of the topic.

It marks a significant shift in focus by looking beyond the language skills developed, and helps students see the academic skills which are developed as part of their language module and how this contributes to the academic and professional skills they acquire as undergraduates. For the first time, the task provides an opportunity for students to evidence their skills.

Selecting Assessment Methods[3] is a particularly useful tool when designing the parameters of a task and the optimum balance. Using this as a guide, the speaking task incorporates the following dimensions:

- **Timing and status**: early in course and summative (end of Semester 1).

- **Topic flexibility**: negotiable, choice of topic and students orient to their own world.

- **Interpersonal**: dialogic and for a public audience.

- **Task engagement**: group and collaborative.

3. https://teaching.unsw.edu.au/selecting-assessment-methods

- **Cost/benefit**: high student workload and significant weighting; low staff workload.

In terms of the linguistic focus, students are aware of the importance of being able to use the language and the opportunities which this presents. Student testimonials reflect their awareness that having good language skills gives them a competitive edge over a candidate with a similar degree and skills set.

3.   Enhancing learning and employability: a brief evaluation

Although the sample of student feedback obtained via a survey was very small, and the limitations of this are recognised, when repeated, a more representative sample will be obtained. Feedback showed that students appreciated the freedom to choose the topic and the opportunity to be creative. They commented that their spoken language and their confidence in using the language had improved. Some also identified progress in their ability to work effectively with others. Only a minority of students used digital media so this requires further investigation to understand how it can be better promoted and supported. Those who did use a digital format commented on their confidence to use digital media. One student wrote: "It pushed me out of my comfort zone so I felt a sense of achievement once it was finished". Applying to their own discipline the skills they have developed on their IWLP module – for example, the student choosing GoAnimate to give a presentation for his Law programme – shows transferability of skills in action. These are skills for learning and for life.

Students who use digital media (see Figure 1) have evidence – linguistic, academic and digital – which they can share by adding a hyperlink to their digital profile. This demonstrates the added value which language modules provide to an undergraduate degree, further enhancing students' employability.

In a review meeting attended by the eight tutors who trialled the assessment, feedback was overwhelmingly positive. While some had initially had reservations about handing over responsibility for the task and the potential negative impact on a student's individual/group mark in the case of poor engagement, they were generally very impressed with the results. For example, using GoAnimate, one group produced a fully scripted, animated debate about racial discrimination in the workplace; another one presented a critical review of the Cannes Film Festival; another presented an analysis of the news using the newsdesk format; others inserted a pre-recorded element within their live presentation.

Figure 1. Screenshot of Kane and Philip's presentation using digital media

Tutors observed that students were more engaged in watching their peers' presentations. This was partly because they were actively listening and concentrating on the quiz designed as part of the task rather than thinking about giving their own presentation, as it had been pre-recorded. The question and answer element is useful in assessing the students' knowledge of the topic and their ability to use the language spontaneously (Klapper, 2006). The results show that presenting a pre-recorded task reduces the nerves normally associated with giving a live presentation, allowing students to perform to the best of their ability. On a practical note, a student who was absent was awarded a mark based on the pre-recorded evidence presented in class – the assessment did not need to be rescheduled and his absence did not have a negative impact on his group.

4.   Conclusion

Re-designing the model of assessment has brought a shift in focus with positive gains for students and staff. The outcomes demonstrate that IWLP modules offer much more than simply language skills – they make a valuable contribution to the knowledge, experience, academic skills, and graduate behaviours which employers expect undergraduates to demonstrate (CBI, 2015) – and using digital media has provided students with evidence.

The next steps involve deciding whether to make the use of digital media a requirement and assess the group interaction, both of which represent new learning outcomes, obtaining employer feedback, and investigating the impact that evidence of their skills has had on the students' employability.

References

Biggs, J., & Tang, C. (2011). *Teaching for quality learning at university* (4th ed.). Maidenhead: McGraw Hill and Oxford University Press.

Boud, D., & Falchikov, N. (2007). *Rethinking assessment in higher education: learning for the longer term*. Oxon: Routledge.

CBI. (2015). *Inspiring growth: CBI/Pearson education and skills survey*. London: Confederation of British Industry. http://www.cbi.org.uk/insight-and-analysis/inspiring-growth-the-education-and-skills-survey-2015/

Elton, L. (1987). *Teaching in higher education: appraisal and training*. London: Kogan Page.

Gibbs, G., & Simpson, C. (2004-05). Conditions under which assessment supports students' learning. *Learning and teaching in higher education, 1*(1), 3-29. http://www.open.ac.uk/fast/pdfs/Gibbs%20and%20Simpson%202004-05.pdf

Klapper, J. (2006). *Understanding and developing good practice: language teaching in higher education*. London: CILT.

12 Enhancing employability skills by bringing literature back into the foreign language class: the Litinclass website

Ana Bela Almeida[1] and Idoya Puig[2]

Abstract

The international research network, 'Literature in the Foreign Language Class' (*Litinclass*), was created with a view of exploring and sharing ideas on the numerous skills and benefits that can be derived from language learning through literature. This paper focuses on how literature can have an important role in the development of specific employability skills in the language class, as it relates not only to purely linguistic abilities, but also helps foster other soft skills such as intercultural awareness, problem-solving abilities and critical thinking. The role of the *Litinclass* research group is also considered, and in particular the *Litinclass* website (https://litinclass.wordpress.com/), in bringing together expertise in this area. This website, aimed at Modern Foreign Languages (MFL) teachers and researchers, both at school and university levels, aims to pool resources and methodologies in the area, and to bring innovation to the study of literature in the foreign language classroom.

Keywords: literature in the MFL classroom, content and language integrated learning, CLIL, new technologies in language learning, employability skills, intercultural awareness.

1. University of Liverpool, Liverpool, United Kingdom; A.Almeida@liverpool.ac.uk

2. Manchester Metropolitan University, Manchester, United Kingdom; I.Puig@mmu.ac.uk

How to cite this chapter: Almeida, A. B., & Puig, I. (2017). Enhancing employability skills by bringing literature back into the foreign language class: the Litinclass website. In C. Álvarez-Mayo, A. Gallagher-Brett, & F. Michel (Eds), *Innovative language teaching and learning at university: enhancing employability* (pp. 105-112). Research-publishing.net. https://doi.org/10.14705/rpnet.2017.innoconf2016.660

© 2017 Ana Bela Almeida and Idoya Puig (CC BY)

1. Introduction: why *Litinclass*?

The international research network *Litinclass*[3] was created with a view of exploring and sharing ideas on the numerous skills obtained and benefits deriving from language learning through literature.

For some time, the value of teaching content and, in particular, literature, was questioned (Edmondson, 1997). Currently, there is a renewed interest in literature which is gradually re-emerging in the language teaching curriculum, as demonstrated in numerous studies (for example Matos, 2012; Paran, 2010; Sell, 2005). Amos Paran (2010), in his book on testing the untestable in language learning (and here the 'untestable' also includes literature), sums up current trends with regards to literature in the language class:

> "although the link between L2 learning and literature may not be as strong as it was in the past, the use of literatures is more prevalent than is commonly thought, and in many cases it never left the language curriculum" (Paran, 2010, p. 6).

As further evidence of this growing interest, we find that the recent changes in the General Certificate of Secondary Education (GCSE) and General Certificate of Education Advanced level (A level) syllabus in schools in the UK show recognition of the importance of literature in the classroom, but more specifically in the language class:

> "Students will be expected to understand different types of written language, including relevant personal communication, public information, factual and literary texts, appropriate to this level" (Department for Education, 2013, p. 4).

---

3. The *Litinclass* research project is coordinated by Dr Idoya Puig and Ms Ana Bela Almeida, lecturers, at the Manchester Metropolitan University and the University of Liverpool, respectively, and gathers collaborators from national (Ms María Muradas-Taylor, University of York) and international (Dr Gonçalo Duarte, University of Paris-Sorbonne 4) universities.

2. The role of literature in intercultural awareness and employability skills

This renewed interest in the teaching of literature in the language class is also related to a move towards a more global vision of language learning. Despite the present context of new technologies and media, the role of literature in language teaching is still unique. Recent studies have been looking at ways of teaching and learning, which, rather than ignoring literature, can utilise new media and technology in teaching without excluding traditional reading skills:

> "Textual literacy remains a central skill in the twenty-first century. Before students can engage with the new participatory culture, they must be able to read and write. Youth must expand their required competencies, not push aside old skills to make room for the new [...]" (Jenkins et al., 2006, p. 19).

Bringing literature back into the language classroom is not, then, an attempt to go back in time. Rather, knowledge of literary texts helps students become better language learners, and provides them with skills that are increasingly necessary in the contemporary globalised world. We propose the following classification of the primary benefits of bringing literature into the language class, as supported by the research and policy documents consulted:

- **Literature enhances foreign language learning**: research has shown that when appropriate student-centred exercises on literature are put into practice in the language classroom, students make more progress in their language learning: "It is clear that literature does have something very special to offer to language learning. [...] It combines attention to meaning with attention to form. [...] It is motivating and engaging" (Paran, 2008, p. 70).

- **Authentic materials increase student engagement with language learning**: literature fosters motivation because "literature provides not only a genuine context for communication; it also gives pleasure by engaging the emotions" (Hill, 1986, p. 9). Also, "literature's contents may well be truer to life and more relevant to learners than the typical textbook topics" (Sell, 2005, p. 15).

- **It provokes discussion of difficult ethical issues:** literature presents the student with human relationships, challenges and dilemmas to be explored and analysed. The study of literature in the language class "serves many more educational purposes – intellectual, moral and emotional, linguistic and cultural – than the purely aesthetic" (Council of Europe, 2014, p. 65).

- **It links with internationalisation, fosters intercultural awareness and provides reflection on diversity and inclusion**: literature offers opportunities to experience different cultures in context. Thus, language classes take on their full potential in the project of cultural mediation: "Language learning helps learners to avoid stereotyping individuals, to develop curiosity and openness to otherness and to discover other cultures" (Council of Europe, 2008, p. 29).

- **It develops important employability skills**: as the job market becomes more and more internationalised, students need to be prepared to engage with different cultural contexts: "At present, students who are extensive travellers demand a different approach to the cultural dimension, which should prepare them to meet and interact with otherness taken in its changing multiplicity" (Matos, 2012, p. 7).

An approach to language learning that enriches students' intercultural awareness will develop important employability skills, preparing students who are enthusiastic and perceptive travellers to engage with cultural diversity:

"Literature written in the target language [...] may give learners insight into other cultures, thus preparing them to act competently and appropriately in future dealings with representatives from those cultures" (Sell, 2005, p. 92).

According to a recent report, *Born Global*, produced by the British Academy (2016) on language skills for employability, in an increasingly competitive job market it is essential that graduates acquire soft skills to communicate with other cultures. The study of languages through literature inherently develops these skills, as specified in the subject benchmark statement:

> "The study of languages enables students to understand the similarities and differences between cultures, in the broadest sense of high culture, popular culture and the customs and practices of everyday life. In this sense it is inherently intercultural" (Quality Assurance Agency, 2015, p. 8).

Literature is an ideal instrument to provide the context to engage with the cultures of the countries where a language is spoken, at the same time as it fosters important skills such as intercultural awareness, problem-solving abilities and critical thinking. These are essential skills for the formation of the ideal transnational graduate of the future, as defined by the British Academy (2016) report.

3. The *Litinclass* website: bringing expertise together

In order to address the challenges and opportunities of exploiting the teaching of literature for all of these purposes, we devised a project to research and explore methodologies in this field. A key tool of the project is the *Litinclass* website, which is aimed at MFL teachers and researchers, both at school and university levels, pools existing resources and also offers original materials derived from our research-led teaching. The website includes the rationale for creating the site and provides links to studies, which highlight the benefits of bringing literature into foreign language studies. It offers a range of activities, which exemplify these benefits and links them to various skills. The project is ambitious and aims to present multilingual resources, linking them more directly to employability skills in particular and to increase the number of collaborators from different countries.

An example of research-led teaching in this field was the successful curriculum review process that took place in an Advanced Portuguese Language module at the University of Liverpool during the academic year 2015/16. More literary texts were introduced in the module, including the reading of a contemporary Lusophone novel. Student activities ranged from text and lexical analysis and creative writing, to the discussion of sensitive issues and even a Skype conversation in Portuguese with the author. Student feedback on the module mentioned that "it's fascinating to learn about the complex interracial relationships of the time" as learned in the novel; and another student stressed that "it is especially appreciated that part of the class focused around a literary text, which helped both our language and knowledge of Portuguese culture". Thus, the students acknowledged that literature helped them develop intercultural awareness, which will make them more sensitive when facing real life situations in their graduate and professional futures. We believe that reading the novel, for example, generated more understanding, empathy and sensitivity and these were manifested in the subsequent analysis of Lusophone culture and current issues in some newspaper articles and other texts. It also fostered a more autonomous response, initiated by the students themselves rather than having to be teacher-led.

4.   Conclusion

Teaching literature in the modern foreign languages classroom means giving students a profound insight into the cultural worlds of the languages they are learning. This is particularly important at a time when we are moving towards offering greater levels of internationalisation in education and post-graduate jobs. The study of literature brings to the classroom employability skills, which underpin professional competence, such as sensitivity to ethical questions specific to a particular culture, critical thinking, respect for cultural values and appropriate responses to these values.

To this end, the *Litinclass* research group will continue to work on creating and sharing resources through the *Litinclass* website. The project is in its early stages but results so far have been promising. We intend to develop more examples taken from classroom practice, to further demonstrate the link between intercultural awareness derived from literature, and the enhancement of specific employability skills.

References

British Academy. (2016). *Born global: a British Academy project on languages and employability*. http://www.britac.ac.uk/born-global

Council of Europe. (2008). *Council of Europe white paper on intercultural dialogue*. http://www.coe.int/t/dg4/intercultural/source/white%20paper_final_revised_en.pdf

Council of Europe. (2014). *Common European framework of reference for languages: learning, teaching and assessment*. http://www.coe.int/t/dg4/linguistic/cadre1_en.asp

Department for Education. (2013). *Modern languages GCSE subject content and assessment objectives.* https://www.gov.uk/government/uploads/system/uploads/attachment_data/file/206148/GCSE_Modern_Language_final.pdf

Edmondson, W. (1997). The role of literature in foreign language learning and teaching: some valid assumptions and invalid arguments. In A. Mauranen & K. Sajavaara (Eds), *Applied linguistics across disciplines. AILA Review 12* (pp. 42-55). Milton Keynes: AILA.

Hill, J. (1986). *Using literature in language teaching*. London: Macmillan.

Jenkins, H., Purushotma, R., Clinton, K., Weigel, M., & Robinson, A. (2006). *Confronting the challenges of participatory culture: media education for the 21st century*. Chicago: MacArthur Foundation. http://www.newmedialiteracies.org/wp-content/uploads/pdfs/NMLWhitePaper.pdf

Matos, A. (2012). *Literary texts and intercultural learning: exploring new directions*. Bern: Peter Lang. https://doi.org/10.3726/978-3-0353-0249-3

Paran, A. (2008). The role of literature in instructed foreign language learning and teaching: an evidence-based survey. *Language Teaching, 41*(4), 465-96. https://doi.org/10.1017/S026144480800520X

Paran, A. (2010). More than language: the additional faces of testing and assessment in language learning and teaching. In A. Paran & L. Sercu (Eds), *Testing the untestable in language education* (pp 1-16). Buffalo: Multilingual matters.

Quality Assurance Agency. (2015). *Subject benchmark statement: languages, cultures and societies*. http://www.qaa.ac.uk/publications/information-and-guidance/publication?Pub ID=2982#.V0LZfuR-5fY

Sell, J. (2005). Why teach literature in the foreign language classroom? *Encuentro, Journal of Research and Innovation in the Language Classroom, 15*, 86-93.

Section 4.

Enhancing employability through digital tools

13 Teachers as awakeners: a collaborative approach in language learning and social media

Alessia Plutino[1]

Abstract

This paper provides an overview of the successful pedagogical project TwitTIAMO, now in its third year, where micro blogging (Twitter) has been used in Italian language teaching and learning to improve students' communicative language skills, accuracy, fluency and pronunciation outside timetabled lessons. It also explores the background and outcomes of two recent implementations to the project: (1) the implementation of a Twitter Champ, acting as a Knowledgeable Other (Vygotsky, 1978) and the development of her transferable employability skills; and (2) the use of a free speech-to-text tool to develop accuracy in pronunciation and writing. More broadly, the paper offers an overview of social media as a powerful tool to transpose classroom communities into online learning communities and enhance spontaneous and collaborative learning outside conventional classroom settings, based on Vygotsky's (1978) Zone of Proximal Development (ZPD) principles and current Personal Learning Environments (PLE) and Communities of Practice (CoP) theories.

Keywords: Twitter, collaborative learning, personal learning environment, communities of practice, CoP, PLE, employability.

---

1. University of Southampton, Southampton, United Kingdom; a.plutino@soton.ac.uk

How to cite this chapter: Plutino, A. (2017). Teachers as awakeners: a collaborative approach in language learning and social media.. In C. Álvarez-Mayo, A. Gallagher-Brett, & F. Michel (Eds), *Innovative language teaching and learning at university: enhancing employability* (pp. 115-125). Research-publishing.net. https://doi.org/10.14705/rpnet.2017.innoconf2016.661

© 2017 Alessia Plutino (CC BY)

1. Introduction

This paper aims to look at one important need for practitioners in today's educational landscape: to understand how we operate in social contexts and engage within our communities in order to make teaching purposeful (Wheeler, 2016).

The advent of Web 2.0 has enhanced students' participation, autonomy and independent learning by generating a collaborative approach based on users' willingness to create and share knowledge, information and user-generated resources within different types of communities.

'Community' becomes an integral part of Web 2.0: the "key idea in the learning-communities approach is to advance the collective knowledge of the community, and in that way to help individual students learn" (Bielaczyc & Collins, 1999, p. 19).

This is also supported by Vygotsky's (1978) social-constructivist theories, which suggest that people learn best through a process of knowledge-construction supported by the community and by Smith's idea that "[w]e learn from the company we keep" (Smith, 1988, in Bielaczyc & Collins, 1999, p. 19).

Vygotsky (1978) states that individuals can learn on their own only to a certain extent and it is with guidance from a More Knowledgeable Other (MKO) that each of us can learn more and achieve a higher potential.

These concepts have nowadays adapted to a wider range of people and situations and MKOs can now be identified with fellow students, colleagues and professional networks.

Besides, being physically present is not anymore the only way to act as an 'MKO': as learning evolves into a collaborative project where the focus is determined by the interest of participants, communities become CoP (Brown, Collins, & Duguid, 1989; Lave & Wenger, 1991) i.e. "groups of people who share a concern or a passion for something they do and learn how to do it better as they interact regularly" (Wenger, 1998, p. 1).

Membership to various CoPs enables students to create their own PLE and students use their networks and external resources to customise and expand their own learning.

After a brief overview of the project, I will explain how the theories cited above have contributed to the implementation of a 'student MKO' to facilitate and enhance language learning using social media (Twitter) and the development of some students' activities.

2. Project overview

The TwitTIAMO project was launched in semester two of the academic year 2013/14 for the Italian ab-initio course at the University of Southampton; a fast paced course, achieving the CEFR B1 level in one year.

The project was a response to students' course evaluation highlighting a gap in terms of Italian cultural awareness as well as tutor's need to provide opportunities for students to improve their communicative language skills, accuracy, fluency and pronunciation outside timetabled lessons. A total of 35 students split in two groups took part in the pilot.

Twitter (a microblogging service with a maximum length of 140 characters per tweet) seemed capable of responding to the combined challenges raised by students and tutor and was therefore chosen for this project after an evaluation of various computer-mediated communication technologies available to students and accessible at any time of the day and from any device.

The fast paced nature of tweets, mimicking spoken language exchanges, seemed to be a good way to evaluate students' communicative language development during out of classroom time.

A public twitter group, TwitTIAMO, was created for the course and administered by the tutor. Students set up their own individual account exclusively for language learning purposes and were asked to follow each other so they could interact outside of classroom time. Few rules were established so that students would get appropriate feedback from the tutor: comments in capital letters would provide correct versions of messages; the tutor would not necessarily reply to all students' tweets but would be selective and choose those which would be beneficial to the whole group. In doing so, the tutor would prompt students to use vocabulary and structures covered in class and facilitate metacognition (Appendix, Figure 1).

3.   Outcomes of the pilot project

The pilot of TwitTIAMO was very popular amongst the 35 participating students. In May 2014, only a semester after its implementation, students nominated the project for an Innovative Teaching Award. The project came first at Faculty level and was highly commended at University level.

A chronological analysis of students' tweets and a cross reference of their written and speaking task performances matched and confirmed previous findings from Ritchie (2009):

- The limit of 140 characters focuses the attention, develops its own sort of discursive grammar set, requiring a great deal of summarising (even synthesising, on occasion).

- Students get a sense of what a person is like outside of the classroom and feel more comfortable with classroom discourse.

- Twitter is purposeful: curriculum-centered but not curriculum-bound.

- It changes classroom dynamics: teachers make themselves available and are connecting their students to the real world, fostering communicative language practice/ research/ cultural full-immersion/ reflection, facilitating communities of users and collaborators.

4.   Phase 2: new implementations

After a successful pilot scheme, the project was rolled over in 2015. Students demonstrated their enthusiasm about being part of a 'community within a community', i.e. a transposed out-of-hours classroom. For this reason, the second phase of the project focused on determining, firstly, whether Twitter could be used to:

- Enhance spontaneous and collaborative learning outside conventional classroom settings based on Vygotsky's (1978) ZPD principles.

- Transpose classroom communities into online learning communities and develop PLEs and CoPs.

Secondly, whether Twitter would allow:

- The implementation of a model which would see a student Twitter Champ gaining and improving a set of specific transferable employability skills whilst liaising with the academic in charge and acting as a Knowledgeable Other for the students participating in the project.

Katie Churchill, (https://pathbrite.com/MlleKC/profile) was chosen as Twitter Champ for her previous enthusiastic participation on the TwitTIAMO project and her affiliation to the wider University multidisciplinary IChamp Network (http://www.diglit.soton.ac.uk/) which helps students develop employability skills by working with academics on digital literacy and cascading their expertise to staff and students. Katie, in teamwork with the tutor, facilitated learning activities by tweeting in Italian about culture and language, acting as a more knowledgeable presence within the Twitter course group.

She ran workshops on Twitter, created user resources, researched apps, solved technical issues, acted as a catalyst for students' engagement and participation and enhanced students' awareness about learning opportunities in social media, exposing them to new online CoP and PLEs.

Her most successful example in this respect was the creation of the Italian Twitter Masterchef challenge, involving students in evening cooking battles practising their Italian. Students were encouraged to become part of a growing community where situated learning was taking place via the process of 'legitimate peripheral participation' (Lave & Wenger, 1991) and belonging to specific CoP.

The second implementation of Phase 2 was more practical in order to determine students' perceptions on:

- Using Twitter for language learning.

- Using speech-to-text tools within Twitter (mobile phone app) as a language learning tool and determine its effectiveness to improve pronunciation and grammar awareness.

A speech-to-text tool allows a user to convert his dictated message into written text.

The Twitter Champ tried and tested various mobile phone speech-to-text tools, however, due to Android vs iOS accessibility issues, her final recommendation was to use the built-in microphone tool that comes with the Twitter app and set the language to Italian.

The aim was for students to 'dictate' tweets rather than write them in the traditional way (Appendix, Figure 2), especially when on the go.

The main pedagogical objective was to activate students' metacognitive skills when using this tool by making different attempts until the spelling on the tweet they were dictating would appear correct.

5.   Conclusion

Although a full data analysis has yet to be completed, interim outcomes seem to confirm previous findings from Ritchie (2009) that microblogging's fast pace and word limit can positively impact on fluency and facilitate interactive discussions, also including reflective learning.

There is an initial indication from students' written and oral performances that those who actively engaged with facilitated activities on Twitter improved their language skills and cultural awareness. The participants' oral and written exchanges showed evidence of a high frequency – and manipulation – of idioms through the use of humour (Appendix, Figure 3). The way idioms contributed to communicative competence and intercultural awareness was also praised by the External Examiner who saw evidence of new and enriched vocabulary, which also confirmed that students had overcome the stumbling block in the acquisition of a foreign language (Kovecses & Szabc, 1996, p. 327).

In terms of topics, although only at beginner level, students were eager and able to discuss controversial issues from various contexts that mattered to them (e.g. exam boycott, Appendix, Figure 4).

The analysis of the students' questionnaires confirmed that the presence of the Twitter Champ helped to facilitate spontaneous discussions and exposed students to 'new horizons' for language learning (Student 12).

The enthusiastic response received by the project is a testimony to the impact of online communities and the difference they can make in teaching by building time and space for communication, discussions and collaboration with others (inside and outside the classroom), to learn more widely (Wheeler, 2016).

In terms of employability skills, the Twitter Champ model established a mutual and productive collaboration between the tutor and the Twitter Champ student.

The latter had numerous opportunities to develop a variety of skills including teamwork, communication, public speaking, self-management, planning and organising. The practical insight into academic environment eventually led Katie to co-present papers at conferences and has undoubtedly been an asset in her successful application for a postgraduate certificate in education.

Finally, with regards to the use of the Twitter built-in dictation tool, the tutor felt this was slowing down the pace, immediacy and spontaneity of Twitter activities. Notwithstanding, 75% of participants found the use of a dictation tool definitely helpful to self-assess their own performances, identify flaws in pronunciation and accuracy, and plan collaborative courses of action, with either a peer or their tutor.

A recommendation can therefore be made to use dictation tools for some specific class or independent activities for those students who particularly need a special focus on self- assessing their accuracy and grammar skills.

References

Bielaczyc, K., & Collins, A. (1999). Learning communities in classrooms: a reconceptualization of educational practice. In C. M. Reigeluth (Ed.), *Instructional design theories and models: a new paradigm of instructional theory, Vol. II.* Mahwah NJ: Lawrence Erlbaum Associates.

Brown, J. S., Collins, A., & Duguid, P. (1989). Situated cognition and the culture of learning. *Educational researcher, 18*(1), 32-42. https://doi.org/10.3102/0013189X018001032

Kovecses, Z. & Szabc, P. (1996). Idioms: a view from cognitive semantics. *Applied linguistics, 17*(3), 326-355. https://doi.org/10.1093/applin/17.3.326

Lave, J., & Wenger, E. (1991). *Situated learning: legitimate peripheral participation.* Cambridge: Cambridge University Press. https://doi.org/10.1017/CBO9780511815355

Ritchie, M. (2009). *Chirping about Twitter.* Times Education Supplement, pp. 18-21.

Smith, F. (1988). *Joining the literacy club.* Portsmouth NH: Heinemann.

Vygotsky, L. S. (1978). *Mind in society: the development of higher psychological processes.* Harvard: Harvard University Press.

Wenger, E. (1998). *Community of practice: learning, meaning, and identity*. Cambridge: Cambridge University Press. https://doi.org/10.1017/CBO9780511803932

Wheeler, S. (2016). #Learning social. *Learning with 'e's*. http://www.steve-wheeler. co.uk/2016/05/learningis-social.html

Appendix

Figure 1.   Example of tutor's reply to help metacognitive reflection

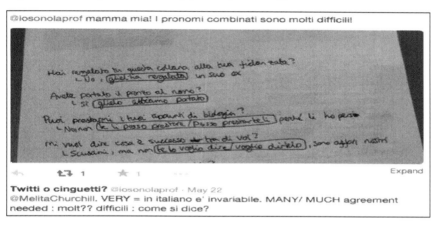

Context

Student was completing a grammar exercise on combined pronouns and posted a picture of her notes.

Translation

Student's tweet: my goodness! Combined pronouns are very difficult!

Tutor's tweet: Very = in Italian it is invariable. MANY/MUCH agreement needed: molt? What is the Italian for this? (Tutor provides an explanation but not the answer).

Figure 2.　Microphone option to 'tweet' on mobile Twitter app

Figure 3.　Example of own made up idiomatic expressions used with humour

Context

Student had been tweeting about what he cooked for dinner. Unfortunately he was missing an ingredient and had to find a substitute.

Translation

Student's tweet: It's no use crying over spilled milk.

Tutor's tweet: this is a nice expression; does it mean that now it is too late to change things and you can only eat salami instead of bacon?

Student's tweet: ah ah! Exactly! I prefer this one: if life gives you lemons, how about making some limoncello?

Figure 4.   Student expressing concern about current affairs: exam boycott

Context

This tweet was posted during a time of academics' industrial action threatening to delay marking for the summer term, with negative consequences on students' graduations.

Translation

Student's tweet: Today I am worried about the marking boycott. I really want to be able to graduate!

14 Enhancing online language learning as a tool to boost employability

Sol Escobar[1] and Susanne Krauß[2]

Abstract

Online learning is a very flexible way to build and improve language knowledge alongside other work and/or study commitments whilst at the same time encouraging autonomous learning, time management, self-motivation and other skills relevant to employability. Learning on your own, however, can also be daunting. Therefore, the Languages for All (LfA) team at the University of Essex have incorporated an innovative blend of tutor support with flexible tailored lessons and bespoke assessments in addition to the Rosetta Stone® Advantage (RSA) programme which is used as the main platform. This combination has contributed to a steep increase in retention and pass rates, placing our modules in an advantageous position. The article presents an innovative (and easily replicable) module structure and – supported by students' voices – shows how learning a language can contribute to enhancing employability.

Keywords: online language learning, employability, eLearning, language learning software, technology enhanced learning, IWLP, independent learning.

1. University of Essex, Colchester, United Kingdom; sescobar@essex.ac.uk

2. University of Essex, Colchester, United Kingdom; skrauss@essex.ac.uk

How to cite this chapter: Escobar, S., & Krauß, S. (2017). Enhancing online language learning as a tool to boost employability. In C. Álvarez-Mayo, A. Gallagher-Brett, & F. Michel (Eds), *Innovative language teaching and learning at university: enhancing employability* (pp. 127-135). Research-publishing.net. https://doi.org/10.14705/rpnet.2017.innoconf2016.662

© 2017 Sol Escobar and Susanne Krauß (CC BY)

1.   Introduction

The number of students learning a language in Institution Wide Language Programmes (IWLP) at UK Universities has seen a steady increase in recent years (UCML-AULC, 2015). LfA, the IWLP available at the University of Essex, allows every student in any degree programme to learn languages at no extra cost on an extracurricular basis during their time at the institution. In addition to traditional face-to-face evening classes, we also offer innovative free online courses in French, German and Spanish. This diverse and inclusive mode of learning has many advantages, such as the flexibility it offers students, the opportunity to balance their language learning with other study commitments, easy access when students are based off-campus and convenience in time and pace of learning. This correlates with student motivations for having chosen the online mode of study[3] as revealed in a survey conducted in 2016[4].

Online learning, therefore, proves to be a flexible way to build and improve language knowledge alongside other work and/or study commitments whilst at the same time encouraging autonomous learning, time management, self-motivation and other skills important in boosting employability.

However, students new to online language learning can find it daunting at first. When we looked into students' previous experiences with online language learning we found that almost 60% of our survey respondents had not learned languages online before, and of the 40% that had, the great majority quoted Duolingo (www.duolingo.com) as their learning tool. Given Duolingo's popularity, this isn't surprising, but it shows that students tend to understand online learning as stand-alone activities rather than structured courses. However, our experience with the Online Portfolio, from its stand-alone beginnings to its current structured design, has shown us that the latter results

---

3. Traditional face-to-face courses in LfA are available only at beginner levels, whereas the Online Portfolio caters for levels up to C1 in the CEFR. Nevertheless, 81% of all students stated the online course was their first choice.

4. 38 Portfolio students participated in the survey conducted and analysed via Qualtrics software https://eu.qualtrics.com/jfe/preview/SV_3Dm2f55o517Bo2x

in better retention, pass rates, and overall successful learning experiences. This article will outline how foreign language learning can help boost employability and how online modules can maximise that potential. We will also describe the module's structure, which could be easily replicated across languages and institutions.

2. Employability and language learning

The Higher Education Academy defines employability as "a set of achievements – skills, understandings and personal attributes – that makes graduates more likely to gain employment and be successful in their chosen occupations, which benefits themselves, the workforce, the community and the economy" (Yorke & Knight, 2006, p. 3). However, detailed information on what these skills, attributes and attitudes entail is much harder to establish. Various surveys and publications[5] on employability make reference to the following:

- Positive 'can do' attitude.

- Aptitude to work.

- Communication skills.

- Problem solving.

- Innovative approach, creativity, risk taking, collaboration.

- Numeracy & IT.

Amongst these, learning a foreign language sometimes features as a separate skill:

---

5. Higher Education Academy (2016); CBI and Pearson Education (2015); Quality Assurance Agency (2012).

"The ability to communicate with other people in their own language can play a valuable part in forming relationships, building mutual understanding and trust, and developing the networks on which business opportunities depend. Language study can also indicate that an individual may have an international outlook and [...] evidence of the ability to work in diverse teams and with other cultures" (CBI & Pearson Education, 2015, p. 41).

Foreign language knowledge and its practical value are increasingly recognised by British businesses: 45% see this as beneficial to their businesses (CBI & Pearson Education, 2015, p. 42).

Knowing a foreign language is not, however, restricted to merely being able to communicate in a foreign tongue. In fact, many of the employability competencies that businesses require are an implicit and integral part of the language learning process, such as cultural awareness, communication skills including learning about English or a mother tongue through the foreign language, teamwork, regulation of self-efficacy and self-management, perseverance, motivation, etc.

But how does this translate into what our students think they gain from such courses? We set out to examine whether students' beliefs about the skills gained through online language learning mirrored those mentioned above, which later informed the changes made to the programme.

2.1.   Students' perspectives on online language learning and employability

Our 2016 survey revealed that student perceptions of the skills gained through online language learning mirror very closely those described by Yorke and Knight (2006) in their definition of employability. This shows us that students are indeed aware that their employability skills, such as autonomy, time management and presentation skills (among others), are being developed alongside their language abilities. In the students' own words:

"I think that especially **autonomy** and **time management** are striking because Languages for All shows my future employer that I am a person who **goes beyond the mere minimum** required and voluntarily engages in extra-curricular activities" (Spanish Portfolio student).

"Being able to give a presentation in a foreign language has **improved my confidence to present in English**" (German Portfolio student).

"[The online course] helped me to **develop an understanding of professionalism** in France [...]. Thus, my professional development has been improved by **expanding my cultural awareness**" (French Portfolio student).

Key areas of impact identified:

- Professional awareness.

- Improved self-confidence.

- Presentation skills.

- Improved language/communication skills in L1.

- More autonomy.

- Time management skills.

- Taking positive actions/extra-curricular engagement.

However, when asked to state the main reason for learning a language, employability ranked very high, but only after 'general linguistic/academic interest' as the top motivator (see Figure 1 below). These results are also mirrored in previous studies from Gallagher-Brett (2004, p. 6).

Figure 1.   Reasons for learning a language[6]

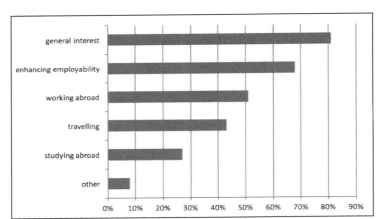

3.   The Online Language Portfolio at the University of Essex: a case study

3.1.   Course structure, content and support

The LfA's Online Portfolio are free extra-curricular courses offered in French, German and Spanish at levels A1 to C1 in the CEFR, and use the RSA[7] software as their content backbone. This technology-mediated method of delivery is then paired with robust tutor support, which we have found to be the most effective combination. Portfolio modules run over two terms with an average of 30-40 hours of tuition and include a face-to-face introduction to the course and software. The tutor then assigns a lesson each week, monitors student progress, keeps them engaged and provides help when needed. The content includes a variety of activities such as short videos, automated speech recognition and automatically graded exercises. The topics focus on 'everyday situations' in the first term, and 'professional situations' in term two, which respond to student's

6. Source: Survey of Languages for All Portfolio Students, 2016, https://eu.qualtrics.com/jfe/preview/SV_3Dm2f55o517Bo2x

7. The Rosetta Stone® Advantage software is specifically designed for higher education. For more information, please visit http://www.rosettastone.co.uk/he-fe/advantage

top two reasons for choosing the course, namely a general interest in the language and employability.

Furthermore, the module is assessed via the progress achieved in RSA as well as one online written and one face-to-face oral assessment. The addition of the speaking test has proven very successful as it adds an element of continuous tutor-student engagement, with learners reporting that an in-person demonstration of their progress at the end of course is a motivator to complete it. Furthermore, upon successful completion of the course, students can apply for the University's employability award, into which LfA has been embedded.

Students are able to maintain contact with tutors via email, Skype or during office hours. The RSA software also offers a customised messaging system, which – through the use of screenshots – enables the tutor to better understand the problem the student might be experiencing and to provide more tailored support. However, while student support is key, it is equally important to provide it in a measured manner. This allows for independent learning to take place and gives students the space to develop skills such as time management and self-reliance.

Additionally, the RSA portal is accessed via the University's learning management system Moodle, which is used extensively across other modules and programmes. This has been purposely implemented to provide a cohesive and uniform academic space, where students can access their extracurricular language course in the same manner they would their other modules. This structure is replicated and consistent across all three language modules, and could be easily applied to online language modules at other institutions by following a similar module organisation.

3.2.   Student feedback and stats

The results of our latest student survey carried out in 2015/16[8] showed that our students were very satisfied with all aspects of interaction with tutors, support,

---

8. 38 students who finished the online modules.

content, skills balance and the variety of activities as well as overall user-friendliness of the RSA software.

As outlined in the Table 1 below, completion and pass rates improved steadily over the past year. This, we believe, is due to the exploration of student needs and the measures we have taken to meet them. These rates are particularly encouraging when we take into account that these are free extra-curricular non-credit bearing academic online courses and that, in comparison, average retention rates for MOOC-like courses are in the region of 15%[9].

Table 1.   LfA completion rates (Essex University)

Completion rates based on overall number of registered students*		
2013/14	2014/15	2015/16
37%	42%	47%
Completion rates based on the number of students active after the first 4 weeks** of the course		
2013/14	2014/15	2015/16
N/A	58%	70%
Pass rates for total active students***		
2013/14	2014/15	2015/16
N/A	79%	90%

*initial number of registrations
**students still registered and attending classes
***those who completed the course

4.   Lessons learned

Online language modules are a useful tool for students to gain language skills alongside other work and/or study commitments while at the same time promoting autonomous learning, time management, self-motivation and other skills relevant to employability. By enhancing these extracurricular language modules we have learned, helped by student feedback, that a combination of independent computer-mediated learning and strong tutor support can be successful in maximising student engagement and improving both retention and pass rates.

9. MOOC completion rates: the data; http://www.katyjordan.com/MOOCproject.html

Through the research described in this paper, we found that paced tutor-student interaction plays a key role, as does monitoring student progress and maintaining flexibility (content, deadlines, etc.) to allow for a more personalised learning experience. The individual format of student-teacher contact helps to maintain levels of motivation high and can also be used to guide students in developing skills, such as time management, which are an asset in the job market. Equally, embedding language courses in university-led employability initiatives, such as award schemes, has proven to positively affect student motivation to take up a language and further enhance self-reflection on its benefits. Finally, we hope that the steps we have taken in the development of these online language modules in order to address diverse and evolving student needs can serve as a model to other educators in the field who might wish to create similar courses.

References

CBI & Pearson Education. (2015) *Inspiring growth: CBI/Pearson Education and skills survey*. http://www.cbi.org.uk/cbi-prod/assets/File/Education-and-skills-survey-2015.pdf

Gallagher-Brett, A. (2004). *Seven hundred reasons for studying languages*. LLAS. https://www.llas.ac.uk/sites/default/files/nodes/6063/700_reasons.pdf

Higher Education Academy. (2016). *Framework for embedding employability in higher education*. https://www.heacademy.ac.uk/enhancement/frameworks/framework-embedding-employability-higher-education

Quality Assurance Agency. (2012) *Enterprise and entrepreneurship education: guidance for UK higher education providers*. http://www.qaa.ac.uk/en/Publications/Documents/enterprise-entrepreneurship-guidance.pdf

UCML-AULC. (2015). *UCML-AULC survey of institution: wide language provision in universities in the UK (2015-2016)*. http://www.aulc.org/documents/UCML_AULC_2015-2016.pdf

Yorke, M., & Knight, P. T. (2006). *Learning and employability, series 1: embedding employability into the curriculum*. http://www.qualityresearchinternational.com/esecttools/esectpubs/yorkeknightembedding.pdf

15 Looking beyond language skills – integrating digital skills into language teaching

Amanda Deacon[1], Lucy Parkin[2], and Carolin Schneider[3]

Abstract

The traditional focus of the language elective has been to give students the skills to communicate in the foreign language which has also been their main selling point. However, language graduates need more specific and wide-ranging skills if they are to compete in the current and future job markets. It is now widely accepted that universities have a direct responsibility to prepare students for employment and, in the 21st century, this preparation needs to include digital literacy and competencies. But how can students not only learn these skills, but also find ways to evidence them for a future employer? At Leeds we decided to explore these issues by designing a new 'Professional French' module, linking digital competencies to assessment through participation on a blog together with supported use of digital media to create presentation videos. This article will discuss how we addressed, with our project, some of these questions and met student demand for more applied options on the French degree programme. We present our experience from the perspectives of the different players: tutor, students, learning technologist, and self-access centre manager, whose Master of Arts (MA) dissertation in technology, education and learning provided the data for the evaluation of this project.

Keywords: employability, collaboration, assessment, digital literacy, digital skills.

1. University of Leeds, Leeds, United Kingdom; a.deacon@leeds.ac.uk

2. University of Leeds, Leeds, United Kingdom; l.parkin@leeds.ac.uk

3. University of Leeds, Leeds, United Kingdom; c.schneider@leeds.ac.uk

How to cite this chapter: Deacon, A., Parkin, L., & Schneider, C. (2017). Looking beyond language skills – integrating digital skills into language teaching. In C. Álvarez-Mayo, A. Gallagher-Brett, & F. Michel (Eds), *Innovative language teaching and learning at university: enhancing employability* (pp. 137-144). Research-publishing.net. https://doi.org/10.14705/rpnet.2017.innoconf2016.663

© 2017 Amanda Deacon, Lucy Parkin, and Carolin Schneider (CC BY)

1. Background

> "Students must start to *live* their CVs before they need to write and market them" (Anyangwe, 2011, para. 5, our emphasis).

Portfolio assessment has been for some time, and still is, part of the French degree and language elective programme at the University of Leeds. The intended advantages are well documented elsewhere: enhancing motivation, building up skills over time and developing student capacity to reflect on their own learning (British Council, 2009).

However, in our experience, students tend to produce work, at best, in the last few weeks of the course and, at worst, just before the deadline. Some students may also adopt a *what-do-I-have-to-do-to-pass?* mentality, possibly reinforced by quality assurance constraints which encourage us to produce ever more transparent and detailed assessment criteria. To counter this, we decided to provide a space where students could take creative risks and address a real audience, opening up the dialogue through broader collaborative engagement within a 'community of practice' (Wenger-Trayner & Wenger-Trayner, 2015). In concrete terms, this meant that students were required to upload drafts of work to a blog (documents, video and audio recordings) and receive feedback from their tutor and peers in preparation for the final submission of the end-of-semester portfolio.

2. Mandy (module tutor)

The project involved 11 students, enrolled on a new level 2 undergraduate French elective module, 'Introduction to Professional French', designed to widen the offer of applied language modules and to embed employability skills. Assessment was by portfolio, presentation, written task, and speaking examination. The blog, hosted on WordPress, was the vehicle used to share written and spoken student drafts and advice on business correspondence: CVs, professional profiles, business letters, telephone calls, and reflections on progress.

In addition to the general project aims stated earlier, we had two primary motivations in designing this module:

- to encourage regular participation and engagement throughout the semester;

- to simulate work practices through on-line collaboration.

To do so effectively, we felt we needed to move away from the limitations of the Blackboard Virtual Learning Environment (VLE) collaborative tools, which only allow plain text comments to blog entries with no facility for hyperlinks or attachments. To do this, we decided to migrate to WordPress, a more user friendly, flexible and visually attractive platform.

We found that student feedback collected in interviews and through surveys (Schneider, 2016a) evidenced the success of our project on several levels.

Students participated and posted regularly, motivated by the assessment criteria which rewarded blog participation, and noted that ongoing feedback could lead directly to improved grades.

There were other interesting findings:

- The blog was seen as a novelty, or as one student put it: "All modules have a VLE but this was different so sometimes I'd just have a look to see what was going on".

- Our students seemed to fear making their work public and were reticent about commenting on each others' posts. This was described variously, in interviews, as being a "bold move" and "not our role". In itself, this was not surprising and in line with other studies focusing on blogging (Bowles, 2016), but interview transcripts also reveal that students dealt with the required peer feedback by negotiating a "sort of agreement" via Facebook so as to avoid the risk of offending each other.

As the tutor, I was learning alongside the students and, on occasion, this caused organisational problems which later had to be rectified by my colleagues. We also discovered, however, that the students themselves were not as technical or digitally literate as we had assumed (Schneider, 2016a). This had advantages and disadvantages. On the one hand, as discussed, the blog had the novelty factor, but on the other, they felt they would have benefitted from some technology specific training. The blog was time-consuming. The very speed of response, which the students valued, and the in-between class participation, which I had hoped for, also meant a fast turnaround for all, with feedback occurring several times a week rather than in a traditional marking cycle. In retrospect, managing student expectations by clarifying when feedback would be posted could have alleviated such pressures.

We had, therefore, achieved our objective of encouraging on-going participation and collaborative work, and also, as intended, enhanced the students' employability. However, as with De Berg's (2016) study, whilst our students recognised and articulated their appreciation of the applied tasks, they did not equate digital literacy and competencies (posting on the blog or making videos) with employability. Nor did they recognise their work as an exportable product that they could show to employers or transfer to other projects (Schneider, 2016a). These soft, or employability, skills and dispositions, sometimes referred to as "wicked competencies", are skills which resist definition and are difficult to assess (Knight, 2007, p. 1). Students, on this module, clearly exhibited these skills through teamwork, negotiation and problem solving, but did not recognise them as such.

3.   Carolin (MA student)

My Master's dissertation in technology, education and learning investigated the impact of the blog on writing and independent learning skills, motivation, and support mechanisms. Data was primarily collected through student questionnaires administered online and on paper, and regular semi-structured interviews with Mandy and three students. Data analysis was carried out using a mixed methods approach, combining qualitative and quantitative instruments to investigate the data for recurring patterns and to ensure relevance, reliability and validity. This allowed me to fully examine the impact the blog had on students' and the tutor's skills development and motivation.

In line with existing literature on the use of blogs in language learning, such as Neira-Piñeiro (2015), Fageeh (2011) and Dippold (2009), my research (Schneider, 2016b) found that the students felt they had developed their language skills and confidence. These were developed alongside other skills (Figure 1). Most students felt that the main skills they had developed were writing and digital literacy skills, while some interviews showed that they did not immediately recognise the skills developed during the module as linked to employability.

Figure 1.   Student skills developed during the module (Schneider, 2016b, p. 36)

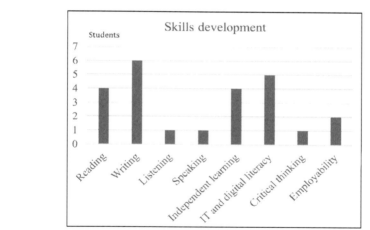

Students stated that they felt motivated to use the WordPress platform to submit homework to their tutor, in part because participation was included in the assessment criteria, but also because they wanted to learn by interacting with each other's work. They saw the platform as an innovative tool, and were aware that the tutor was learning alongside them.

It appears that Mandy and the students, although appreciating the mutual support mechanisms developed during the module, required more structured and ongoing assistance to fully benefit from using a blogging platform for language learning. With this in mind, I suggest that adequate technical support needs to be put in place to allow the tutor to develop her digital skills, so that in the future she will be able, in turn, to support her students and to facilitate the use of technology for learning more effectively. Similarly, it is suggested that the students' skills and needs are assessed in the module induction.

4.   Lucy (learning technologist)

I am member of the blended learning team, and have a Master of Science (MSc) in multimedia and e-learning. My perspective is also that of a former language learner. I feel that, since my own undergraduate degree in 1999, little has changed and that language teaching and learning has not kept pace with digital advances and technology. I would like to see the language electives draw students away from a limited horizon of linguistic competence to developing a portable and transferable product; something they can 'show off' or showcase in the next stage of their career. My vision is that the blog would become a simulation of a Francophone business magazine with a wider audience rather than just a tutor and their students. The mode of delivery would, then, move from the current tutor led version to one where students themselves research and present articles on how to approach the required tasks for the portfolio and publish their findings as blog posts.

As discussed, the project was successful. However, looking to the future, we need to address the three most surprising student responses revealed by Carolin's research:

- initial low level of digital competence;

- failure to recognise digital and soft skills as valuable for their professional profiles;

- reticence to critique each other's work due to a perceived risk to the group dynamic.

To achieve this, technical support for tutors and students needs to be put in place by our blended learning team. In addition, the students' digital skills should be audited at the start of the module and a skills workshop, tailored to their needs, should be scheduled for the first week of the course. Activities will be planned to help students to recognise and evidence their less tangible employability skills to future employers. Finally, we will explore on-line socialisation (Salmon, n.d.) as a tool to facilitate constructive peer feedback.

5.   Conclusion

Working together has allowed us to exchange ideas, resources and skills from academic and non-academic viewpoints. Through this project we have participated in several overlapping but distinct forums or communities of practice (Wenger, 1998) involving students, a tutor, a learning technologist, and a researcher, all of which have allowed us to develop our own practice while enhancing the learning and teaching experience.

References

Anyangwe, E. (2011, April 4). What are you doing to improve the employability of your graduates? *The Guardian*. https://www.theguardian.com

Bowles, E. (2016). Blogging in humanities teaching. In *Forum issue B3*. https://goo.gl/r3CTHr

British Council. (2009). *Portfolios in ELT*. https://www.teachingenglish.org.uk/article/portfolios-elt

De Berg, A. (2016). Students as producers and collaborators: exploring the use of padlets and videos in MFL teaching. In C. Goria, O. Speicher, S. Stollhans (Eds), *Innovative language teaching and learning at university: enhancing participation and collaboration* (pp. 59-64). Dublin Ireland: Research-publishing.net. https://doi.org/10.14705/rpnet.2016.000405

Dippold, D. (2009). Peer feedback through blogs: student and teacher perceptions in an advanced German class. *ReCALL, 21*(1), 18-36. https://doi.org/10.1017/S095834400900010X

Fageeh, A. I. (2011). EFL learners' use of blogging for developing writing skills and enhancing attitudes towards English learning: an exploratory study. *Journal of Language and Literature, 2*(1), 31-48.

Knight, P. (2007). *Fostering and assessing wicked competencies*. http://www.open.ac.uk/opencetl/sites/www.open.ac.uk.opencetl/files/files/ecms/web-content/Knight-(2007)-Fostering-and-assessing-wicked-competences.pdf

Neira-Piñeiro, M. d. R. (2015). Reading and writing about literature on the internet: two innovative experiences with blogs in higher education. *Innovations in Education and Teaching International, 52*(5), 546-557. https://doi.org/10.1080/14703297.2014.900452

Salmon, G. (n.d.). *The five stage model*. http://www.gillysalmon.com/five-stage-model.html

Schneider, C. (2016a). *Using and supporting a blog for teaching French for professional purposes*. Unpublished raw data.

Schneider, C. (2016b). *Using and supporting a blog for teaching French for professional purposes*. Master's thesis, University of Leeds, England. https://bumsonseats.wordpress.com/

Wenger, E. (1998). *Communities of practice: learning, meaning, and identity*. New York: Cambridge University Press. https://doi.org/10.1017/CBO9780511803932

Wenger-Trayner, E., & Wenger-Trayner, B. (2015). *Communities of practice: a brief introduction*. http://wenger-trayner.com/introduction-to-communities-of-practice/

Author index

19813906R00096

Printed in Poland
by Amazon Fulfillment
Poland Sp. z o.o., Wrocław